EMPIRE OF THE SUN

EMPIRE OF THE SUN

PLANETS AND MOONS OF THE SOLAR SYSTEM

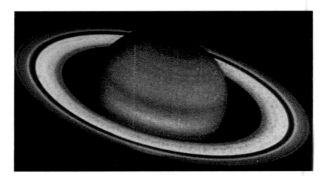

JOHN GRIBBIN & SIMON GOODWIN

NEW YORK UNIVERSITY PRESS
Washington Square, New York

First published in the U.S.A. in 1998 by
NEW YORK UNIVERSITY PRESS
Washington Square
New York, N.Y. 10003

Library of Congress Cataloging-in-Publication Data
Gribbin, John R.
    Empire of the sun : planets and moons of the solar system / John
Gribbin & Simon Goodwin.
        p.   cm.
    ISBN 0-8147-3117-1
    1. Solar system – Exploration.   2. Planets – Exploration.
3. Astronautics in astronomy.   I. Goodwin, Simon, 1971–
II. Title.
QB501.5.G75   1998
523.2 – dc21   98-21564
                                                            CIP

Printed in Hong Kong

CONTENTS

....

ACKNOWLEDGEMENTS

....

Thanks to Jonathan Gribbin for electronic image processing and invaluable advice on layout and design.

All pictures are courtesy of NASA except for the following. Page 25, © Jeremy Maris; Page 19, R. Beebe (NMSU) and NASA; Plate 3, courtesy of SOHO/UVCS and EIT consortia; Plate 4, courtesy of SOHO/EIT consortium (SOHO is a project of international cooperation between ESA and NASA); Plate 16, SeaWiF project, NASA; Plate 49, R. Albrecht (NASA/ESA Space Telescope European Coordinating Facility) and NASA; Plate 50, A. Stern (SwRI), M. Brie (Lowell Observatory), NASA and ESA.

AUTHORS' NOTE

This book follows the standard scientific practice in using the (American) billion of a thousand million (1 000 000 000), not the (British) billion of a million million (1 000 000 000 000).

Distances across the Solar System are usually given by astronomers in terms of the average distance between the Earth and the Sun, which is defined as one astronomical unit (1 AU). In round numbers, 1 AU = 150 million kilometres (about 93 million miles). Since light takes 499 seconds to cover this distance, this distance can also be referred to as 499 light seconds, or 8.3 light minutes.

Following a common astronomical usage, we use terms like 'geology' and 'geological' to refer to the study of planets other than the Earth – for example, the geological activity of Venus.

INTRODUCTION

In 1997, while the spaceprobe Galileo was sending back spectacular images from the planet Jupiter and its moons, a tiny robot explorer crawled around the surface of Mars, the Mars Global Surveyor spacecraft went into orbit around the planet, and, towards the end of the year, the Cassini probe blasted off for the ringed planet Saturn. This flurry of activity was part of the beginning of the second wave of the scientific exploration of the Solar System by unmanned craft, after a gap of nearly ten years since the probe Voyager 2 sent back images from Neptune, across 5 billion kilometres of space.

The first phase of this investigation of the Solar System had begun in 1959, when a probe launched by the Soviet Union flew past the Moon. In the same year the first photographs of the far side of the Moon, never seen from the surface of the Earth, were obtained. Over the next thirty years, culminating in the Voyager 2 flyby of Neptune in 1989, every planet in the Solar System (with the exception of Pluto, which is a peculiar object that should not really be classified as a planet at all) was visited by at least one probe. But though this transformed our scientific understanding of the nature of those planets and their moons – as well as providing spectacular images from the surfaces of these distant worlds – that whole era of planetary exploration should never be seen as anything more than a reconnaissance. To put it in perspective, after this first reconnaissance we had images of the other planets only slightly better than the views of the Moon that Galileo saw when he first turned a telescope on its surface, early in the 17th century. The hiatus that followed was accidental, a result of a combination of factors. The changing political situation, with the break-up of the Soviet Union; economic factors; a shift of emphasis from 'pure' science to obtaining a better understanding of the planets in order to help solve problems, such as global warming, here on Earth; and, not least, the *Challenger* disaster, which delayed the departure of the Galileo probe for years, and led to a rethink of many aspects of the American space programme. But now that the second wave of exploration of the Solar System has begun, the data and images from the old probes are proving useful once again, providing a set of benchmarks against which the new observations can be compared. How would we know, for example, that some of the moons of Jupiter have changed since the 1980s, if the two Voyager probes had not been there in the 1980s? And, thanks to the dramatic improvements in computer power and image processing techniques in the past ten years (let alone since 1959), some of the old images have been processed in new ways, to produce both improved scientific data and even more spectacular visual delights.

(Opposite) The farthest human beings have yet ventured into space is our nearest neighbour, the Moon. This photograph shows an Apollo 17 astronaut driving the Lunar Rover in the Taurus–Littrow Valley.

Our aim in this book is to focus unashamedly on the visual delights, offering you our selection of the best vistas of the Solar System that have yet been unveiled. We use some images from the first wave of planetary exploration (but usually dressed up in new, digitally enhanced finery), many from the new wave of planetary probes, and some from our old friend, the Hubble Space Telescope, which provides the best images we can get from Earth orbit of the other members of the Solar System. Of course, there will be more, and more spectacular, images to come, from the future probes that will explore Mars in more detail, from Cassini, and from missions that have yet even to reach the drawing board, let alone leave it. But that is no reason not to take stock now of the incredible variety of objects in our immediate cosmic neighbourhood. They really only have one thing in common: their membership of the Solar System. They are all gripped in the gravity of the Sun, which dominates its subjects more than any great emperor in history ever dominated his subjects. The Empire of the Sun extends from the Sun itself out beyond even the orbit of Pluto, literally halfway to the nearest stars, where a cloud of frozen, icy bodies – the comets – is held in place by the Sun's gravity. We have images for you in this book of every kind of object known to exist in the Solar System, from the Sun itself to those comets, from planets to moons, and including the lumps of cosmic rubble known as asteroids.

But though our aim is primarily to entertain you with these breathtaking images, and to share with you our delight at the wonders they reveal, we shall not neglect the scientific side of the story entirely. When new discoveries are made in science, either by observation or as the result of new experiments, the observers or experimenters generally have mixed feelings about the way they want things to turn out. On the one hand, it would be nice if our cherished theories and ideas about the Universe were confirmed by the new observations and experiments. On the other hand, it would be exciting to discover something new and unexpected, which could form the basis of a better understanding of the Universe – or, at least, of one small corner of the Universe. The discoveries that have been made over recent decades about our Solar System – the Empire of the Sun – manage to please on both counts. The details have been astonishing and surprising. Nobody imagined for one moment that the moons of Jupiter, for example, would be so different from one another, or that some of them would be so geologically active. There are actually erupting volcanoes on Io, one of those moons, the first volcanoes to be seen erupting anywhere other than on Earth. Explaining the details of the new discoveries – exploring what amounts to a new Solar System – will keep many astronomers busy for at least another generation.

At the same time, though, the broad picture that has been revealed by the exploration of the Solar System so far confirms and strengthens our understanding of what the Solar System is, and how it came into being. In our previous book, *Origins*, we touched on this in the context of the cosmological understanding of where the Universe itself, and the stars and galaxies within the Universe, came from. It is a stunning achievement of the human intellect to be able to say, with confidence, that the Universe had a definite beginning, and

(Opposite) From close orbit around the Earth, the thinness of the smear of atmosphere that supports life is clearly visible (*see also* Plate 14).

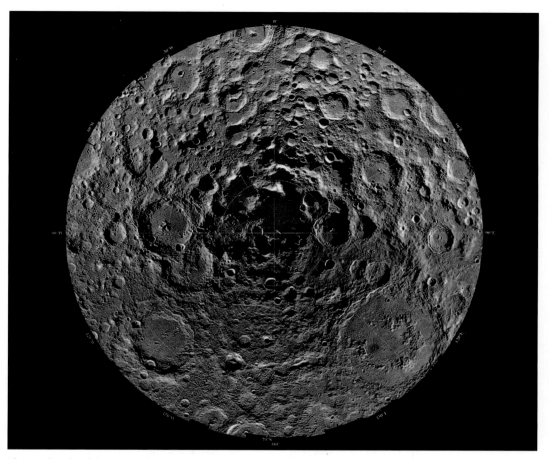

The south pole of the Moon, shown in a mosaic of images obtained by the Clementine spaceprobe.

that this was between 13 and 15 billion years ago. But it is scarcely less stunning, by any everyday standards, to be able to say that the Solar System (including the Earth) had a definite beginning, and that it occurred about 4.5 billion years ago. So, to put the images you are about to see in context, we want to spell out in a little more detail this thorough modern understanding of how the Solar System formed, an account that has been amply confirmed by what the spaceprobes have found. Then we can give you at least a flavour of the mysteries remaining to be investigated when we deal with the individual planets and moons.

The Sun itself is a star – and a pretty ordinary star at that. It formed when a cloud of gas and dust in space collapsed, probably as a result of a large, nearby star exploding as a supernova. The collapsing cloud was almost certainly (judging from the clouds we see collapsing in this way in the Milky Way today) big enough to have formed dozens or hundreds of stars broadly similar to our Sun. These stars have gone their separate ways over the past few billion years and are now lost among the hundred billion stars of the Milky Way, the Galaxy in which we live. The cloud was chiefly composed of hydrogen and helium gas, left over from the Big Bang in which the Universe was born; but crucially,

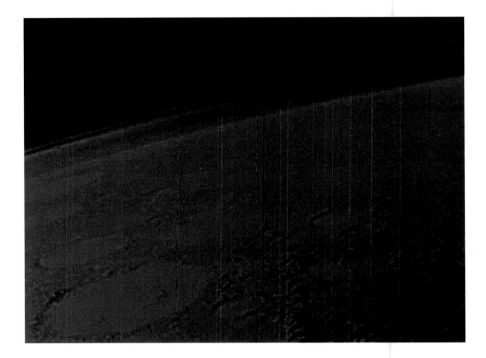

The striking difference between Mars and Earth is brought out by comparing this Viking Orbiter image with the blue Earth in Plate 14. A thin haze of carbon dioxide crystals can just be picked out in the atmosphere.

during the time since the Big Bang several previous generations of stars had run through their life cycles, and laced the interstellar medium with the debris ejected in their death-throes. The nuclear reactions that keep stars shining during their lifetime work by fusing together nuclei of hydrogen to make more helium, and by successively sticking helium nuclei together, thereby building up elements such as carbon, nitrogen and oxygen. Other elements, such as uranium and lead, are manufactured in supernova explosions. Every element on Earth except the primordial hydrogen and helium has been manufactured inside stars and spread through space in this way; and the only reason that the Sun has a family of planets, including the Earth, made out of heavier elements is because it is a relative latecomer to the cosmic scene.

The Sun is a ball of hot gas (strictly speaking, a ball of plasma) which contains about 330 000 times as much mass as the Earth, in a sphere roughly 109 times as big in diameter as the Earth. It is made up of 71 per cent hydrogen by mass, and 26 per cent helium, with a smattering of heavier elements. The Sun makes up 99.86 per cent of the mass of the Solar System – everything else put together, all the planets, moons and cosmic rubble, makes up the remaining 0.14 per cent, and two-thirds of that is locked up in one planet, Jupiter.

With all this weight crushing inwards, the density at the heart of the Sun is twelve times that of solid lead (160 times the density of water), and the temperature is about 15 million degrees (on the absolute, or Kelvin scale, where the freezing point of water is 273 K; for all

The Sun, ruler of the Solar System, shown here in an ultraviolet image obtained from Earth orbit during the Skylab missions.

practical purposes, the temperature at the heart of the Sun can be thought of as 15 million degrees Celsius). Under these extreme conditions, even though the core of the Sun is so dense it behaves like a perfectly fluid gas. In the core, energy is released by nuclear fusion, as hydrogen nuclei are converted into helium nuclei. Along the way, each time a

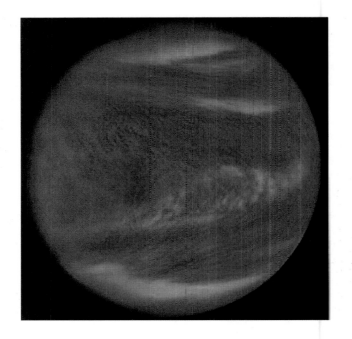

The sulphuric acid clouds of Venus, photographed by the Venus Orbiter probe in ultraviolet light.

helium nucleus is made in this way a little mass is converted into energy, in line with Einstein's famous equation $E=mc^2$. Overall, to hold up the Sun against its own weight and keep it shining steadily, about 5 million tonnes of matter is converted into pure energy (ultimately, into sunlight) each second. Burning fuel at this prodigious rate, the Sun has lost about 4 per cent of its original stock of hydrogen over its 4.6 billion year lifetime to date. This energy emerges, in the form of light, from the visible surface of the Sun, which is at a temperature of about 6000 K. But, as we shall see, the Sun itself extends beyond the visible surface, in the form of tenuous streamers of gas reaching out into space, and even beyond the orbit of the Earth.

The planets can be divided neatly into two groups of four, each group made up of planets with similar properties to those of the other members of the group, and various kinds of cosmic rubble. A ninth object, Pluto, is usually called a planet for historical reasons. In fact, it is a rather large piece of cosmic rubble, more like a comet than anything else. We shall follow historical convention and dignify Pluto with the honorary title of 'planet', but we do not include it in our overall description of how the real planets formed. The two groups of planets whose origins need explaining are the four small, rocky objects (known as the terrestrial planets) which orbit close to the Sun, and the four large, gaseous planets (the gas giants) which orbit farther out from the Sun.

Mercury is the closest planet to the Sun. It orbits the Sun once every 87.97 days, at an average distance of 0.39 AU. So when Mercury is exactly between us and the Sun, its distance from the Earth is only 0.61 AU; when it is on the opposite side of the Sun, it is 1.39 AU away (but can't be seen, of course, because the Sun is in the way). It has no

The Mars Global Surveyor spaceprobe sent back this detailed image of part of the surface of Mars soon after it went into orbit around the red planet in September 1997. It shows part of a feature called Nirgal Vallis. Because of problems adjusting the orbit of the spacecraft, it will not begin its full mapping mission until March 1999; then it will send back images showing features ten times smaller than the smallest shown here.

atmosphere, a diameter of 4880 km (intermediate in size between the Moon and Mars) and a mass one-twentieth that of the Earth.

Venus is the next planet out from the Sun, and comes nearer to the Earth than any other planet. It orbits the Sun once every 225 days at an average distance of 0.72 AU, so at its closest to us it approaches to 0.28 AU from Earth. It has a very dense atmosphere, chiefly carbon dioxide, a diameter of 12 104 km, and 82 per cent as much mass as the Earth.

The Earth itself is, as we all know, a rocky planet with a thin atmosphere and the only oceans of liquid water on any planet in the Solar System today. It is, by definition, at a distance of 1 AU from the Sun, and takes one year (365.26 days) to orbit the Sun once. It has a diameter of 12 756 km, and a mass of just under 6 thousand billion tonnes. The most distinctive astronomical feature of the Earth, though, is its relatively enormous Moon, which is the biggest in proportion to its parent planet of any moon in the Solar System (again, not counting Pluto as a planet). In many ways, the Earth–Moon system resembles a double planet, rather than a planet and its moon. Our Moon has a diameter of 3476 km and a mass 1.2 per cent of the mass of the Earth. It was formed long ago, when

(Opposite) The best views of Mars we can get from Earth orbit come from the Hubble Space Telescope. This image was obtained on 25 February 1995, when Mars was 103 million km from Earth.

the Solar System was young, when an object at least the size of Mars collided with the Earth.

The collision generated so much heat that the entire surface crust of the Earth melted, and great globs of molten rock were flung into space, where they coalesced and formed the Moon. This model of the formation of the Moon explains why its composition is almost identical to the composition of the surface rocks of the Earth, and why it contains scarcely any water, which was all boiled away by the heat of the impact (the Earth's water is thought to have come from deep within the planet, released by volcanoes over geological time). The whole collision process can be modelled very accurately in a computer.

The last of the terrestrial planets is Mars. It orbits the Sun once every 686.98 days, at a distance varying between 1.38 and 1.67 AU. It has a very thin carbon dioxide atmosphere, a diameter of 6795 km and a mass just over one-tenth the mass of the Earth (less than ten times the mass of the Moon).

Beyond the orbit of Mars there is a region, from about 1.7 to 4 AU from the Sun, in which many pieces of cosmic rubble orbit the Sun in a ring, rather like the rings of Saturn but on a much larger scale. The orbital periods of these objects, the asteroids, are between 3 and 6 years. It is estimated that there are more than a million of them which are each at least a kilometre across in this ring of cosmic debris, plus many more smaller objects. Asteroids whose orbits are accurately known are given numbers, and many also have names. The largest of the asteroids, or minor planets as they are sometimes called, is Ceres, with a diameter of 933 km; but only ten minor planets (including Ceres) are bigger than 250 km across. The asteroids are the remains of failed planets that were prevented from coalescing and forming planets when the Solar System was young, but were smashed into one another by the gravitational pull of Jupiter, disturbing their orbits. But most of the

Jupiter, viewed by the spaceprobe Voyager 1 as it approached the giant planet early in 1979. The moon Io can be seen in front of the face of Jupiter, just below centre right of the picture.

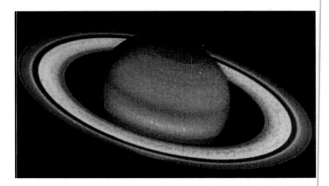

Saturn, viewed by the Hubble Space Telescope in September 1990. Although this was before the flaw in the optics of the HST was corrected, this highly detailed image was produced by combining three separate images of Saturn from the Wide Field and Planetary Camera and using computer enhancement to bring out the detail.

original mass in the asteroid belt has been lost, as objects have been ejected by Jupiter's gravity, perturbing them into orbits that sent them crashing into the other planets (including the collision that formed the Moon), or out of the Solar System altogether. Today, the total mass of all the asteroids in the belt put together is only about 15 per cent of the mass of the Moon.

Jupiter itself, the first and grandest of the gas giants, lies beyond the asteroid belt at a distance of 5.2 AU from the Sun. It orbits the Sun once every 11.86 years. It has a diameter 11 times that of the Earth, and a mass 0.1 per cent that of the Sun, more than twice as much mass as all the other planets, moons and bits of rubble in the Solar System put together. Jupiter has its own mini-empire, a family of at least 16 moons (there may well be further small ones awaiting discovery) and a faint ring system. Unlike the terrestrial planets (but like the other gas giants), Jupiter is mainly composed of hydrogen and helium gas. It is more like a failed star than a planet in the terrestrial sense.

Saturn orbits the Sun at a distance varying between 9 and 10 AU, taking 29.46 years to complete each orbit. It has a diameter at the equator 9.4 times the diameter of the Earth, and a mass 95 times the mass of the Earth. Like Jupiter, it is accompanied by a family of moons; it also has a spectacular ring system, one of the visual highlights of any tour of the Solar System.

Uranus, the seventh planet out from the Sun, orbits at a distance varying between 18.3 and 20.1 AU, taking 84 years to complete each orbit. It has a diameter just over four times that of the Earth (modest for a gas giant) and a mass 14.5 times that of the Earth.

Neptune, the farthest real planet from the Sun, orbits once every 164.79 years, at a distance of 30.06 AU. Since it was only discovered in 1846, this means that astronomers have not yet had the opportunity to watch one complete orbit of Neptune around the Sun; no doubt they will find a suitable way to mark the occasion, in 2011, when the first observed orbit is completed. Neptune has a diameter 3.8 times the diameter of the Earth, and a mass 17.2 times that of the Earth, so it is very similar to Uranus. Both Uranus and Neptune have large families of moons.

Pluto is a planetary wanderer, discovered in 1930, with a highly elliptical orbit which varies between about 30 AU (taking it closer to the Sun than Neptune) and 50 AU. At its farthest, light from the Sun takes seven hours to reach Pluto. It has a mass only 0.3 per cent that of the Earth (about twice that of our Moon), and a moon, Charon, which is more than half as big as Pluto and orbits at a distance of only 19 400 km (for comparison, our Moon orbits the Earth at a distance of 384 400 km). Pluto and Charon are both probably icy chunks of debris typical of a swarm of pieces of cosmic icebergs that litter the region of space beyond the orbit of Neptune. This ring of iceberg-like supercomets is called the Kuiper Belt.

Far beyond the Kuiper Belt lies the Oort Cloud, a spherical shell of cometary icebergs surrounding the Solar System, between about 50 000 and 100 000 AU from the Sun, so distant that light takes one and a half years to get from the Sun to the Oort Cloud. But even this far out into space, in the far reaches of the Empire of the Sun, the comets are still held in orbit around the Sun by gravity. The cloud may contain as many as 100 billion comets, each one an icy lump travelling in a long, slow orbit around the Sun. From time to time, something (perhaps the nearby passage of another star) will shake some of these comets loose, and send them falling in towards the Sun on orbits that will take millions of years to bring them in to our part of the Solar System.

There, the heat from the Sun boils away gas from the comet, often producing a spectacular tail of tenuous material that shines in reflected sunlight as the comet swings around the Sun and heads back into the depths of space. Sometimes, comets are trapped by the gravity of Jupiter and diverted, like the famous Halley's Comet, into orbits that bring them swinging through the inner Solar System every few decades. In 1997, the spectacular visit of Comet Hale–Bopp to the inner Solar System reminded us all of the beauty of these objects; together with the impact of Shoemaker–Levy 9 with Jupiter in 1994, Hale–Bopp also reminded us that occasionally during the long history of the Earth our planet has been struck by one of these visitors from space, wreaking terrible devastation. The death of the dinosaurs, 65 million years ago, is thought to have been caused by just such an event.

But how did the planets and comets (and the rest of the cosmic rubble) get there in the first place? The explanation takes us back to the birth of the Solar System, as just one localised collapsing region of a larger cloud of collapsing gas and dust, squeezed into collapse by the blast wave from a nearby supernova, 4.6 billion years ago.

As far as the existence of the planets is concerned, the key feature of the Solar System is the way material is organised in a thin disk, with essentially all of the material in the disk moving the same way around the Sun. When the cloud that collapsed to form the Solar System started to collapse, it must have been rotating, if only a little – it would be an extraordinarily unlikely cloud that just hung in space without rotating at all. As that cloud collapsed, the rotation would have got faster and faster, just as spinning ice-skaters spin faster if they pull their arms inwards. The relationship between how fast an object is spinning, how big it is and how massive it is, is measured in terms of a property called angular momentum, and angular momentum alone would have been able to stop the spinning cloud contracting, holding it up against gravity, so the Sun would never have formed – unless some of the angular momentum could be got rid of.

Cosmic rubble. Three asteroids, photographed separately by the Galileo spaceprobe, put together as a montage by NASA.

Obviously, the 'protosun' did get rid of enough angular momentum, or we would not be here pondering these puzzles today. This happened partly because the protosun ejected material into space, carrying angular momentum away with it, and partly because some of the material in the cloud settled into a disk around the young star. Angular momentum depends on how far the mass concerned is from the centre of rotation, as well as the amount of mass and how fast it is moving. So Jupiter, even though it is much less massive than the Sun, carries a great deal of angular momentum because it is not only big (for a planet) but far from the centre of the Sun. And the other objects in the Solar System also help to store angular momentum that would otherwise have prevented the Sun from forming at all.

In the disk of the Solar System, all the planets (including Jupiter) orbit the Sun in the same direction. Most of the planets have moons, and with very few exceptions the moons orbit the planets in the same direction that the planets orbit the Sun (the exceptions are thought not to be original moons, formed *in situ* when the Solar System was born, but lumps of rubble captured by their parent planets at a later date; one might call them foster moons). Even the rotation of the planets is turning them on their axes in the same

The far side of the Moon. Never seen from the Earth, the far side of the Moon was imaged by the Galileo spaceprobe as it set off on its voyage to Jupiter. The colouring in this image indicates the different kinds of surface material present at different places on the Moon (*see also* Plate 22).

direction (with the exception of Uranus and Venus, which may have had their spin changed by impacts with large pieces of cosmic rubble). And the Sun itself, turning on its axis once every 25.3 days, rotates in the same direction again. All this is powerful evidence that the planets and (most of) the moons did form at the same time as the Sun, out of a thin disk of material thrown out from the collapsing protosun. The material in the disk condensed to form planets, and for the larger planets the whole process repeated in miniature, with families of moons growing up around those planets in the same way that a family of planets grew up around the Sun.

The easiest thing to explain, on this kind of picture, is why there are two kinds of planet in the Solar System – small, rocky planets near the Sun, and large, gaseous planets farther out. It was all thanks to the heat of the young Sun, which blew the more volatile material away from the inner regions of the Solar System, leaving it to condense out farther from the Sun, where the temperature was lower.

Planet-building must have begun in the original gas cloud before material had even started to form a disk around the protosun. Tiny grains of dust in the cloud would have collided with one another and stuck together to make fluffy supergrains, each a few millimetres across. Because these grains were constantly being bombarded by molecules of gas in the increasingly dense collapsing cloud, they would have been very susceptible to the processes which transfer angular momentum, and would have settled quickly into the disk (literally being pushed into place), giving them ample opportunity for further interactions with one another.

At first, the stickiness of these supergrains was what mattered – they would collide together rather gently, because they were all moving in the same direction around the Sun in the disk, so they would not be disrupted in the collisions and would join together. By the time these primordial pebbles had grown to about the size of asteroids, perhaps a kilometre or so across, their own gravity would have become important, tugging groups of asteroids together in swarms, encouraging collisions and interactions which made bigger and bigger lumps. But head-on collisions, which would have disrupted the lumps, were rare, because everything was moving in the same direction around the Sun. The bigger lumps, with the strongest gravitational influence, then swallowed up the rest of the rubble in their immediate orbital vicinity, sweeping a clean path around the Sun. Those larger lumps became the planets – and as we shall see, the evidence of this final 'sweeping up' process is clearly visible on the battered faces of planets and moons today.

As the objects that were to become the planets grew in this way, the young Sun was glowing at the heart of the cloud of gas and dust in which they were forming. Close to the Sun, the heat was enough to drive out any material that was easily volatilised, so the growing clumps of matter were dominated by substances that are not easily volatilised, such as iron and silica. Farther out from the Sun, though, the original grains from the interstellar cloud that collapsed to form the Solar System would retain a coating of icy material, including water-ice, frozen methane and frozen ammonia. And as large lumps of material started to accumulate far out from the Sun, their gravitational pull was sufficient to trap some of the hydrogen and helium being blown out from the heart of the original gas cloud by the activity of the young star at its centre.

Beyond the orbit of Jupiter, there must have been a huge amount of this frozen stuff, forming very many ice-balls. Some of these icebergs accumulated to form what became the inner cores of the other giant planets; but the gravitational influence of Jupiter itself soon dominated what went on in this region of the disk. Some of the ice-balls were diverted into orbits taking them close by the Sun, where they evaporated entirely after a few orbits. Others smashed into the inner planets (there is a school of thought which says that this is where most of the Earth's water came from, with only a 'topping up' from volcanic eruptions). But many were deflected outwards, in a kind of gravitational slingshot effect, where they formed the Kuiper Belt and the Oort Cloud.

A recent calculation, based on computer simulations of this process, suggests that there was initially about 120 Earth masses of icy material in the region beyond Jupiter and within the present-day orbit of Neptune. Of this, 85 Earth masses went to make the cores of Saturn, Uranus and Neptune, with gas accreting onto those cores by gravity. So 35 Earth masses of primordial material was left over in the form of cometary icebergs. Half were perturbed into orbits taking them close by the Sun, and 16 Earth masses of cometary material went the other way, being ejected from the Solar System entirely to roam interstellar space. Just 1.5 Earth masses of material was left to form the Oort Cloud. The Solar System was complete, and the boundary of the Empire of the Sun had been defined.

And all of this was a natural consequence of the collapse of a cloud of gas in space, laced with a smattering of dust in the form of interstellar grains – dust that had itself been formed out of elements forged in the nuclear furnaces of previous generations of stars. There is no reason to doubt that every time a star forms in this way it will be accompanied by a retinue of planets not unlike the Solar System. Very many stars, as it happens, do not form in isolation in quite this way: they form multiple systems, with two or three (or more) stars in orbit around one another. But whenever a star does form in isolation— and that means many millions of stars in the disk of the Milky Way alone, even allowing for them being a small minority of the stellar population – planets like those in our Solar System must form as well. In all probability, this means that life – even intelligent life – may be quite common, and that at this very moment there are other civilisations exploring other planetary worlds, and marvelling over the images being sent back to their home planet.

The Empire of the Sun is special to us, but it is surely not unique. As we sit back and enjoy a guided tour of the best views in the Solar System, it is worth keeping in mind the possibility that one day this may all seem as parochial as a medieval European map of 'the world', bounded by the Mediterranean Sea and the Atlantic Ocean, with more distant regions simply marked 'Here be Dragons'.

(Opposite) Comet Hale–Bopp, photographed here from the surface of the Earth using an ordinary 35 mm SLR camera, passed through the inner Solar System in 1997. The spectacle provided by the comet's two tails, clearly visible here, was the result of heat from the Sun boiling material away from the dirty ice-ball that formed the nucleus of the comet (*see* Plate 30).

THE PICTURES

PLATE 1

SUNRISE FROM APOLLO 12

For many people, the first time they began to have any true feeling for the fragility of our home in space came at the end of the 1960s, when the Apollo missions brought back the first images of the Earth as a planet. Our tour of the Solar System begins with the Sun, which sits at the centre of its planetary empire; but it also begins with the Earth, the oasis in space on which we live. This simple but striking image was obtained by the astronauts of Apollo 12 on their journey home from the Moon in November 1969. It shows the Sun just emerging from an eclipse, when the Earth passed directly between the returning spacecraft and the Sun. The thinness of the atmosphere – the life zone of our planet – is dramatically highlighted by this view, and rainbow-like stripes of colour can be seen at either end of the arc of atmosphere illuminated by the rising Sun.

PLATE 2
A SOLAR FLARE, SEEN FROM SKYLAB

On 19 December 1973, during the third and last manned Skylab mission, the astronauts in orbit around the Earth witnessed one of the most spectacular solar flares ever recorded. The arc of ionised gas (plasma) sent climbing into space by this event spanned more than 588 000 km, about one and a half times the distance from the Earth to the Moon. This photograph was taken in light at the extreme ultraviolet part of the spectrum, at wavelengths too short to be visible to human eyes, produced by energetic helium atoms. Active regions on the surface of the Sun show up as bright patches at these wavelengths.

This kind of activity comes and goes with a rhythm roughly 11 years long, known as the solar cycle. The Sun was building towards a peak of activity, due at the end of the 1990s, while we were preparing this book.

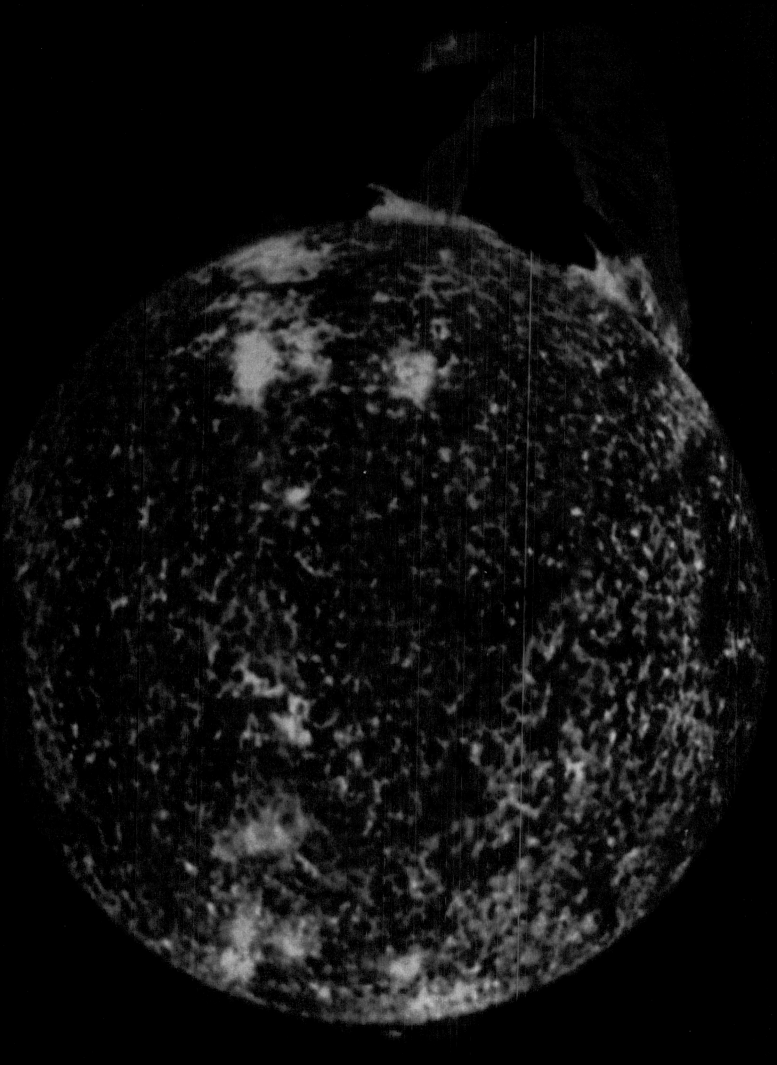

PLATE 3

THE OUTER REGIONS OF THE SUN

Because the surface of the Sun is so bright, neither the human eye nor cameras can detect the relatively faint atmosphere of the Sun, except during an eclipse, when the Moon conveniently blocks out the light from the Sun itself. Borrowing a trick from nature, astronomers make artificial eclipses by placing a disk of material, just big enough to obscure the main image of the Sun, in front of their detectors. In this composite image obtained by detectors on board the unmanned SOHO spacecraft, one detector has looked directly at the Sun, while a separate detector has simultaneously observed the outer atmosphere by using the artificial eclipse technique. The two images have then been put together to give a picture of how hot material streams away from the surface of the Sun and out into space in all directions.

The surface of the Sun itself and its lower atmosphere (inside the dark circle) are seen here in the ultraviolet light emitted by highly ionised (electrically charged) iron atoms, at a temperature of 2 million degrees Celsius; the outer atmosphere is seen by the light of ionised oxygen atoms, at a temperature of 200 million degrees Celsius, escaping into space. The composite image clearly shows that the hottest and most active (brightest) regions in the escaping gas are directly above the active (bright) regions on the solar surface.

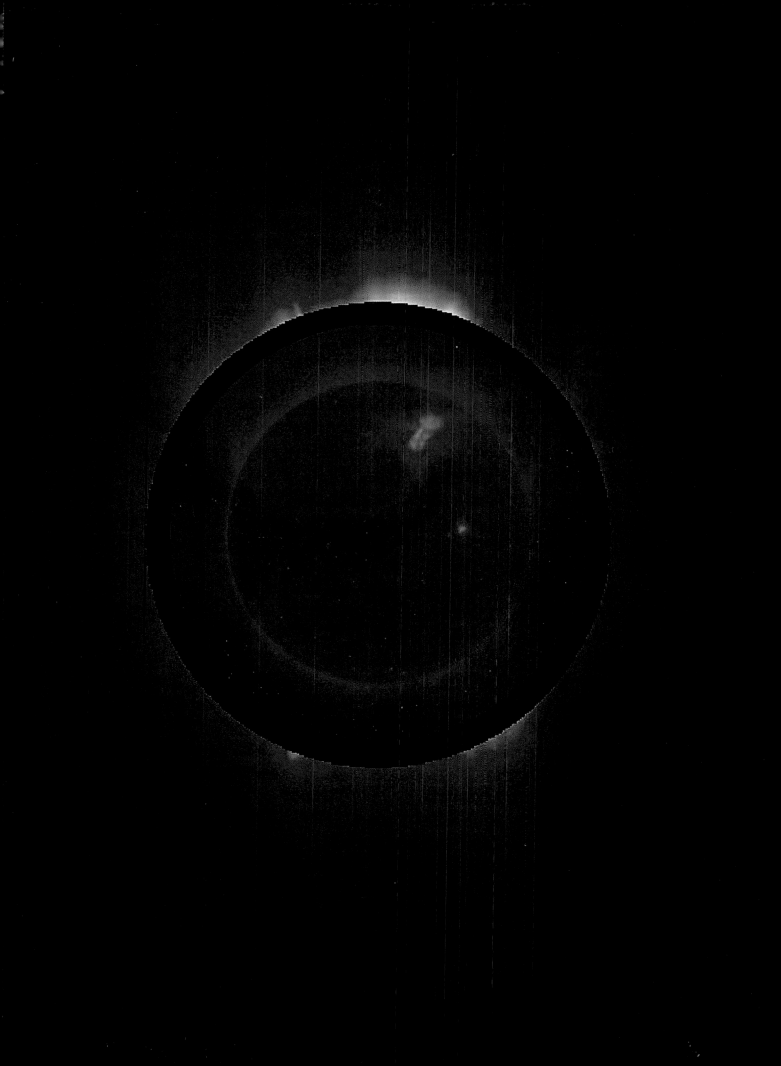

PLATE 4

SOLAR BLUES

Everyone has heard of a 'blue Moon' – but a blue Sun? This image is, strictly speaking, a 'false colour' view since no human eyes could ever see the light that was used to obtain it, in the extreme ultraviolet region of the spectrum, bluer than the bluest visible light. It was taken by an instrument on board the SOHO probe, as part of a sequence that shows the dynamic activity of the ever-changing surface of the Sun (even when the Sun is at a relatively low level of activity overall) as a movie recorded in real time. The activity that is imaged in this way is seen in the thin atmosphere of the Sun, the region known as the corona which lies just inside the dark circle in Plate 3, where the temperature reaches more than a million degrees Celsius and produces intense ultraviolet radiation from atoms of iron which have been stripped of many of their electrons.

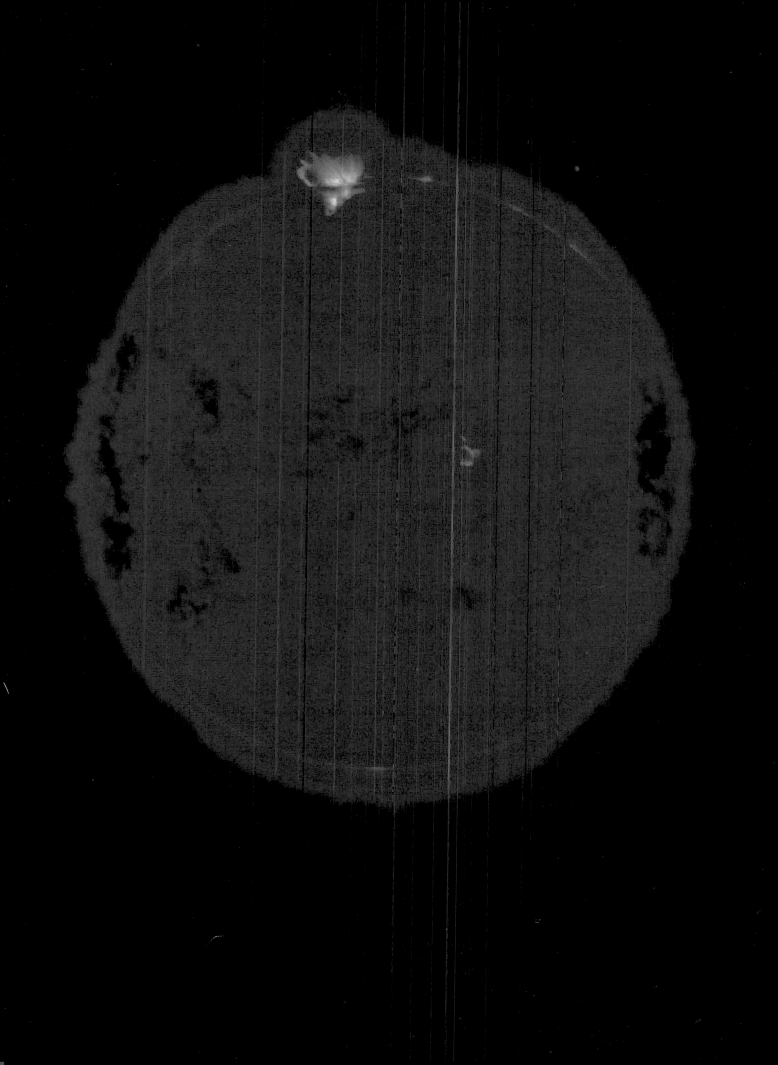

PLATE 5

MERCURY

....

Mercury is the closest planet to the Sun. This makes it very difficult to study using telescopes on Earth, because when the planet is on the same side of the Sun as us we can only see its night side, while when it is on the other side of the Sun it is hidden in the glare of the Sun itself. The first time astronomers had any idea what the surface of Mercury was like was when the spaceprobe Mariner 10 made the first of three flybys past the planet in 1974. The face of Mercury turned out to bear a striking resemblance to the surface of our Moon, with many craters bearing witness to the battering it had received when the Solar System was young. This was one of the key pieces of evidence which helped to establish the modern understanding of the formation of the planets, outlined in the Introduction.

This mosaic of Mariner 10 images gives a good impression of the overall appearance of Mercury, even though you can see the joins where individual photographs have been put together. Colour has been added to highlight the surface features.

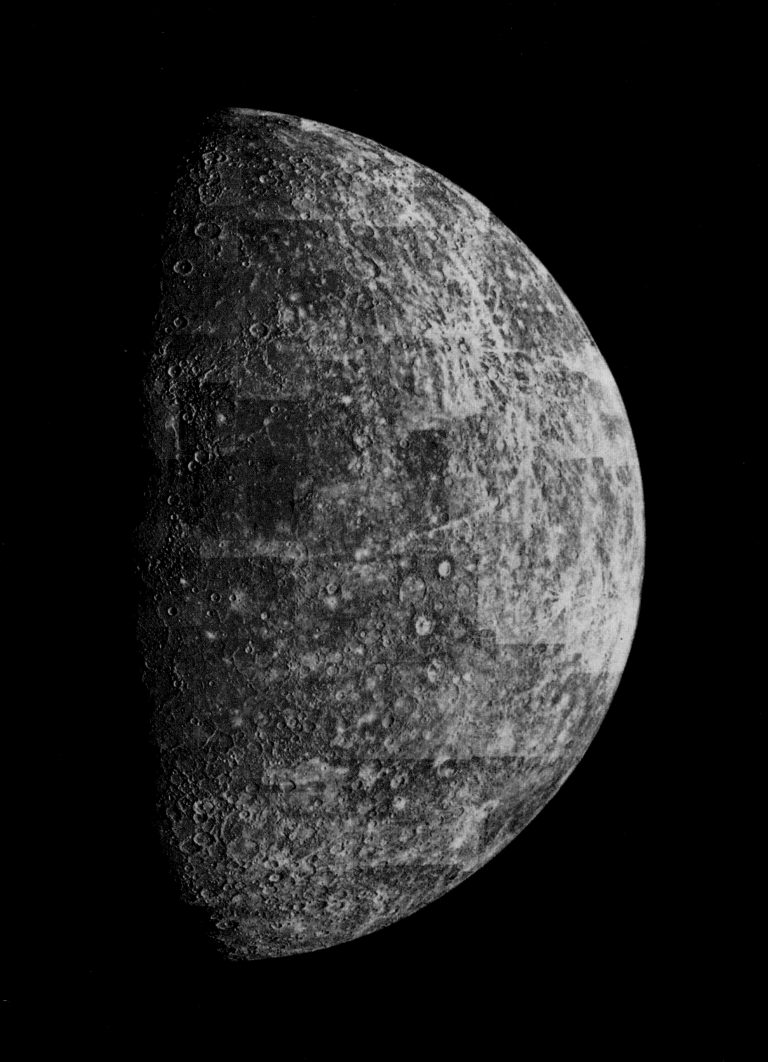

PLATE 6

MERCURY IN CLOSE-UP

Although Mariner 10 was one of the first wave of spaceprobes to open up our understanding of the Solar System, no subsequent probe has since visited Mercury. So the best images we have of the surface of the innermost planet are all two decades old and, as this close-up shows, lack the crisp detail of some of the other images in this book. Nevertheless, close-ups sent back by Mariner 10, like this one, are invaluable because they show no sign of volcanoes or other geological activity. It is quite clear that Mercury is a dead planet, and that the craters on its surface were made by impacts long ago, not by volcanoes. Very little has happened on the surface of Mercury for more than 3 billion years.

The colour that has been added to this image may give a more accurate idea of how the planet would look to the human eye.

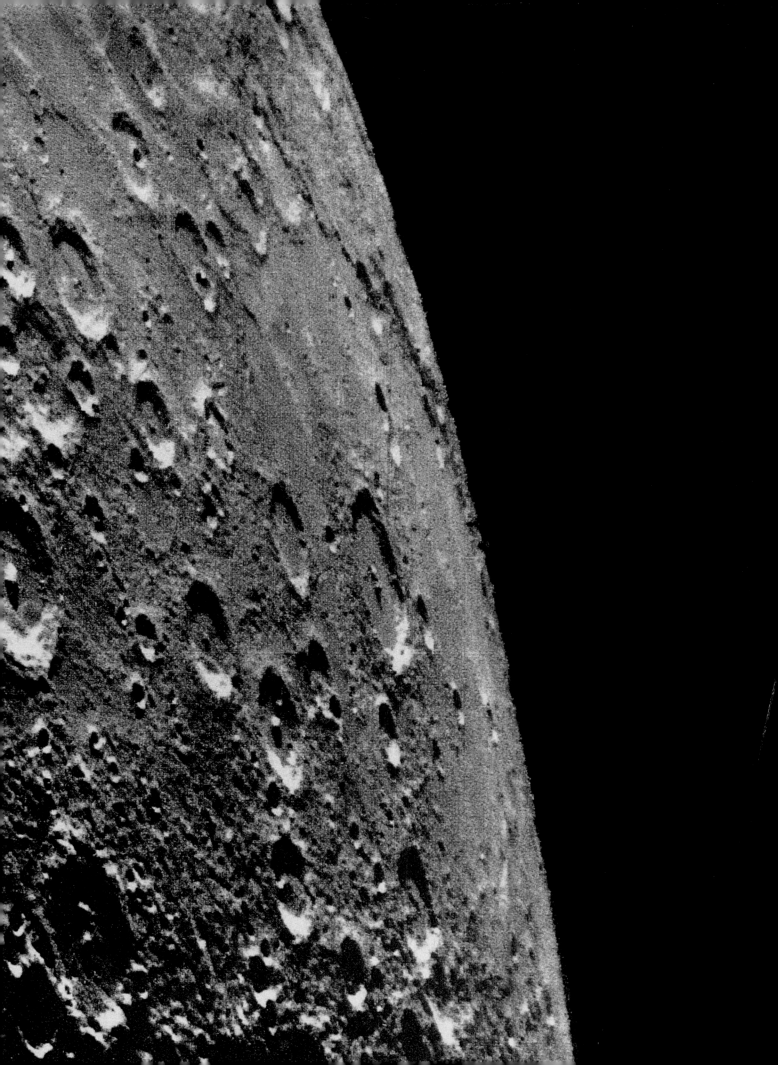

PLATE 7

THE CLOUDS OF VENUS

If Mercury is difficult to observe, Venus is an Earth-based astronomer's nightmare. As well as lying between us and the Sun, which raises the same observational problem as posed by Mercury, unlike Mercury Venus is covered by a thick atmosphere and swathed in clouds. So even a passing spaceprobe cannot obtain a direct image of the surface. This picture, taken by the probe Galileo from a distance of 2.7 million km in February 1990, highlights the problem. All we can see are the sulphuric acid clouds, streaked by their rapid westward movement at speeds of up to 100 metres per second.

Had any human astronauts been on board Galileo, they would not have seen even this much detail. To human eyes, the clouds of Venus are a featureless white smear. The structure in this photograph has been revealed by taking it through a violet filter, and then colouring the resulting image blue to enhance the contrast.

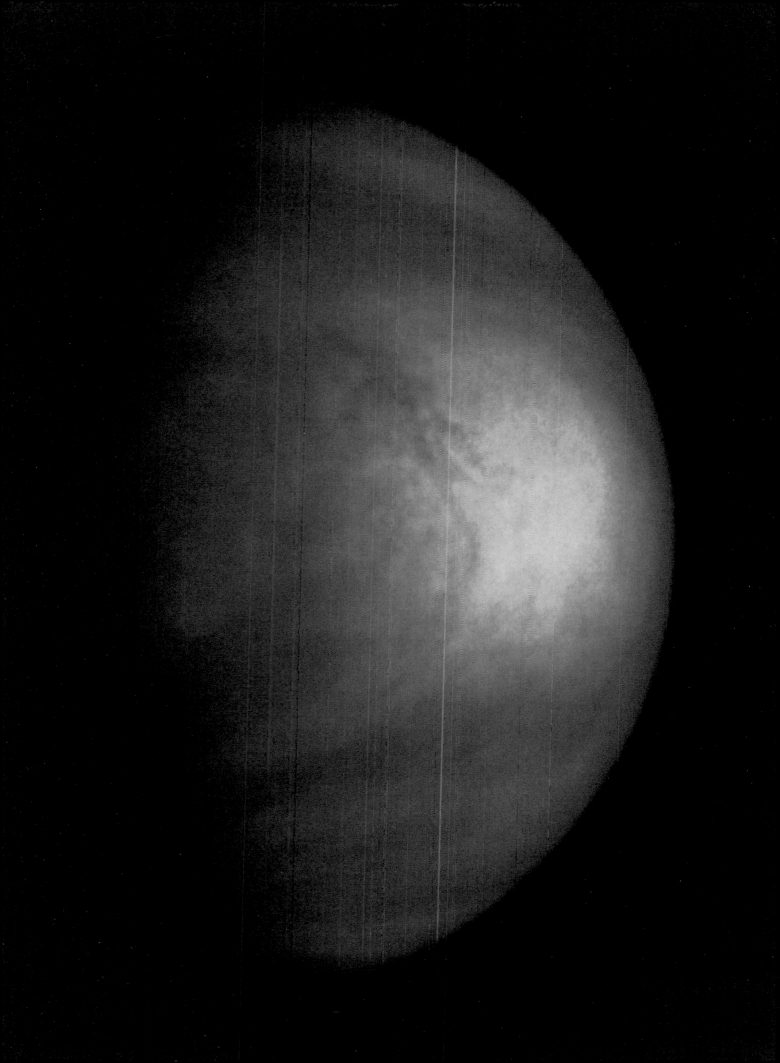

PLATE 8

THE SURFACE OF VENUS

The only pictures we have from the surface of Venus were obtained by the Soviet Venera probes in 1982. Venera 13, which reached the surface on 1 March 1982, sent back fourteen pictures, including this one, during the 2 hours and 7 minutes that it survived before being simultaneously cooked, crushed and corroded by the heat, pressure and acid rain. This colour image was obtained by combining information from three images taken through dark blue, green and red filters; it is a panoramic view, covering 170 degrees, with part of the spacecraft visible at the bottom of the photograph. Part of the horizon has been cut off by the angle at which the camera scanned. The object on the ground in the foreground is a lens cover from one of the cameras.

Although the picture clearly shows both rocks and soil on the surface of Venus, it is difficult to judge what the true colour of this material is, because the atmosphere of Venus filters out blue light. But the images from Venera 13 (and its companion probe Venera 14) provide the best guide we have to what the colour of the surface of Venus would be if the obscuring atmosphere and clouds were stripped away.

PLATE 9

PROBING VENUS'S SURFACE

Although visible light cannot penetrate the clouds of Venus, radar can. Astronomers first bounced radar signals from Earth off Venus in the 1960s, and began to get information about its surface topography that way. In the 1970s, the NASA probe Pioneer Venus and two Soviet probes, Venera 15 and Venera 16, went into orbit around Venus, and used radar to probe its surface in more detail. But the veils of Venus were finally ripped away by the Magellan probe, which went into orbit around Venus in 1990, and used radar to map almost the entire surface in such detail that it revealed features only 100 metres across. By combining these topographic maps with colour information about the surface rocks from the Venera 13 and 14 missions, astronomers have been able to produce computer-generated virtual reality images of how the surface of Venus would look if it were not obscured by cloud; some of these stunning images are shown on the next few pages.

The most striking overall feature of the surface of Venus is that, unlike Mercury, it is clearly an active planet where geological processes continue to the present day. This particular image shows pancake volcanoes, produced by lava oozing out from molten layers below the surface of the planet and spreading across the surface. The domes are about 25 km across and 750 m high, and are shown as if they were being viewed from an altitude of 2.4 km. The vertical scale has been exaggerated in this image to bring out the detail of these structures.

PLATE 10

A VENUSIAN VOLCANO

This is an example of the detail that is present in the Magellan radar data. The image, which covers an area of about $250\,000$ km^2, is centred on an unnamed volcano that is about 2 km high. The colours have been chosen to indicate the temperature of the rocks around the volcano, red corresponding to high temperatures and blue to (relatively) low temperatures.

This kind of volcano is common on Venus, and bears a clear family resemblance to the shield volcanoes of the Earth – classic cone-shaped structures like the volcanoes of Hawaii.

PLATE 11

COUNTING CRATERS

As well as its geological activity, the surface of Venus is also scarred by many large impact craters. This view is of a group dubbed the 'crater farm', and is made up of Saskia (37.3 km across, in the foreground), Danilova (47.6 km across, to the left) and Aglaonice (62.7 km across, to the right). Once again, the topographic detail comes from Magellan, and the colouring is based on data from Veneras 13 and 14.

Images like this help to confirm that the inner planets of the Solar System have been battered by cosmic impacts. But a comparison of the number of craters visible on the face of Venus and the number visible on the surfaces of other planets shows that something spectacular happened to Venus about 600 million years ago. There are far fewer craters on Venus than there would be if, like Mercury and the Moon, it had retained its original scarred surface layer. From the counts of craters, astronomers infer that the surface of Venus was wiped clean in some geological upheaval that completely resurfaced the planet with fresh lavas about 600 million years ago, and that this may have been only the most recent of several such events in the planet's 4-billion-year history.

This focuses alarmingly on the continuing impact threat in the inner Solar System today. It implies that all of the cratering seen on the face of Venus now, including the 'farm' opposite, has happened in the relatively recent geological past, and that objects big enough to cause craters as large as these still roam the inner Solar System. The Earth, as well as Venus, is at risk from such objects, and has also been subjected to a similar bombardment from space over the same sort of timescale – as the dinosaurs discovered to their cost.

Tantalisingly, the resurfacing of Venus occurred at about the time of the first great diversification of life in the oceans of the Earth, after billions of years of stagnation. Nobody knows if this is anything more than a coincidence.

PLATE 12

VENUS IN PERSPECTIVE

Like Plate 10, this perspective view of a region of Venus known as Sedna Planitia has been colour-coded to indicate the temperature of different regions of the surface. The low-lying regions of Venus are marked by several features like this, in which depressions surrounded by fracture patterns (known as coronae) form lines along the planet's tectonic belts (not unlike the volcanic 'ring of fire' that bounds the Pacific Ocean on Earth). It is thought that the coronae are caused by 'hot spots' beneath the surface of Venus, which first push magma up and lift the surface, then cool and contract so that the surface slumps into a depression and the surrounding rocks crack in this distinctive way. Sometimes the lava escapes onto the surface; it can be seen in this image as bright flows of material in the image.

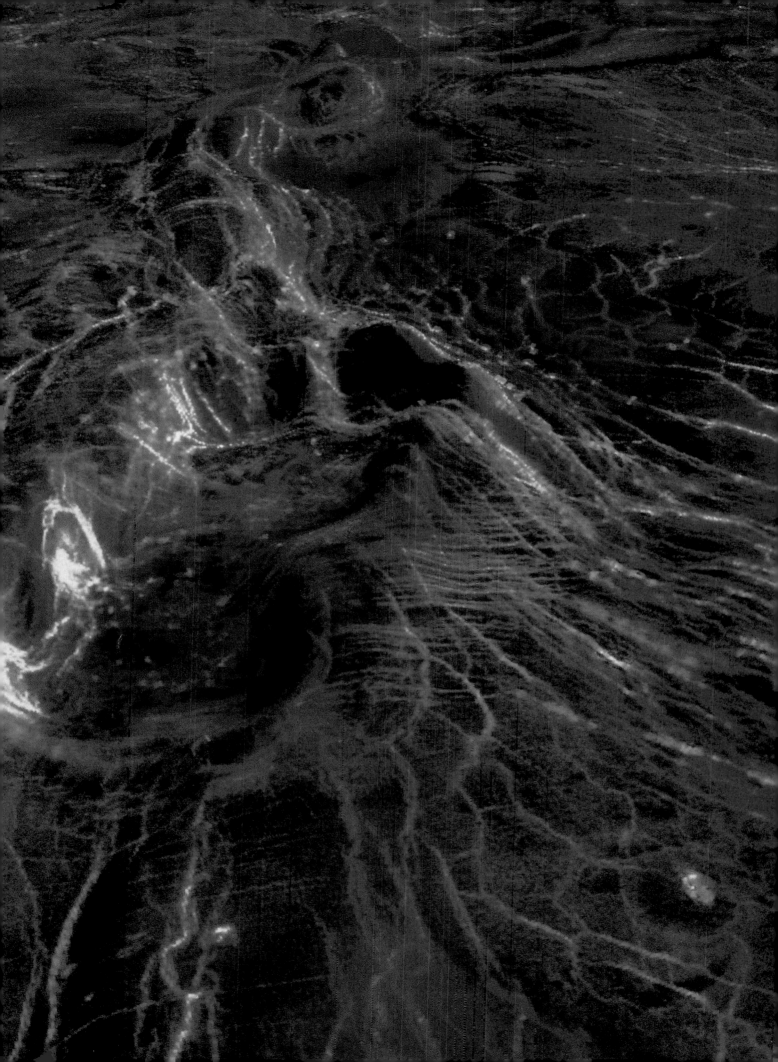

PLATE 13

VENUS UNVEILED

Many years of work went into producing this image of one hemisphere of Venus as it would appear if the planet had no atmosphere. Most of the data used to make it come from Magellan, which sent back data from Venus from 1990 to 1994; but gaps have been filled in with radar imagery and altitude information from Pioneer Venus, from Veneras 15 and 16, and even from ground-based radar studies made using the Arecibo radio telescope in Puerto Rico. Imagery from Magellan itself covered more than 98 per cent of Venus at a resolution of about 100 m; the smallest features visible in this mosaic are about 3 km across. The colours in this image are not intended to represent the true colour of the surface of Venus, but are coded to indicate the varying elevation of the surface (rather like a colour contour map) and to emphasise contrast.

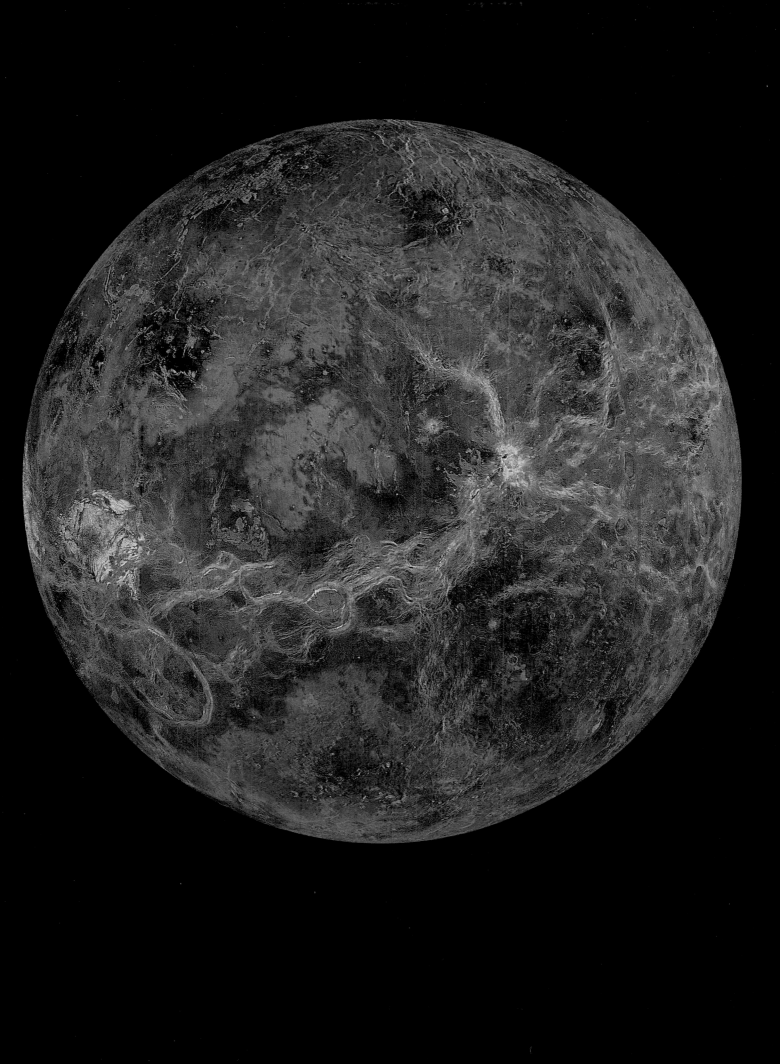

PLATE 14

OASIS EARTH

The image of the fragile Earth floating in space like a beautiful blue marble, with a scarcely discernible skin of atmosphere maintaining the life zone around our planet, has become a cliché of the space age. Cliché or not, the image is barely 30 years old, dating from the Apollo missions of the late 1960s; and it does convey a genuine sense of our place in the Universe, putting human civilisation with its hopes, fears and conflicts in a cosmic perspective. This particular photograph of the nearly full Earth was taken by the astronauts of Apollo 15, and shows South America just left of centre. Central America, Mexico and Florida can be seen at the upper left, while Spain and northwest Africa are visible at the upper right. The image was taken on 26 July 1971 from a distance of 50 000 km, four times the diameter of the Earth.

PLATE 15

GLOWING IN THE DARK

Like the other planets of the Solar System, the Earth has also been studied using electromagnetic radiation from parts of the spectrum not visible to human eyes. These studies are revealing details of how the atmosphere works, and are improving our understanding of features such as climatic change and depletion of the ozone layer. This is a far-ultraviolet image, obtained during the Apollo 16 mission, on 21 April 1972. The 10-minute exposure was taken using a filter to block out ultraviolet light from atoms of hydrogen, but allow through light from oxygen and nitrogen, the two main components of our atmosphere. The colour has then been tweaked, as usual, to bring out details of the image. Although the atmosphere glows most brightly on the sunlit side of the Earth, where it is energised by the light from the Sun itself, airglow emission can also be seen on the night side of the planet.

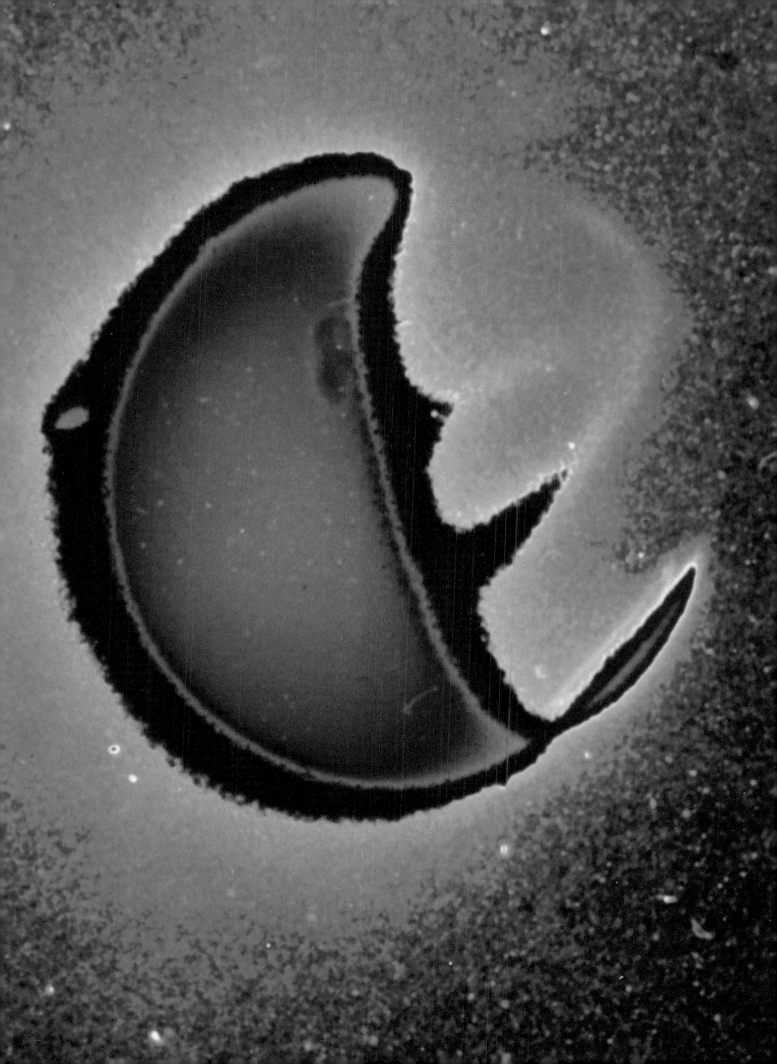

PLATE 16

LIFE ON EARTH I

The importance of observations of the Earth from space is highlighted in this dramatic picture, obtained using data from the satellite SeaWiFS (a tortuous acronym derived from Sea-viewing Wide Field-of-view Sensor) in September 1997. Several images have been combined to give a view of the Earth 'unwrapped', as in a conventional map projection. The aim of this was to map the different concentrations of marine organisms known as phytoplankton in the world's oceans. The more phytoplankton there are, the greener the water looks. As a bonus, the image also shows the pattern of vegetation across the land surface of the planet; but one of the most striking features is the pall of smoke spreading over south-east Asia, from the forest fires that devastated Indonesia at that time. These fires were started by farmers and forestry workers to clear land, but raged out of control for weeks, producing an environmental catastrophe across the region.

PLATE 17

RANGING WITH RADAR

To put the radar-derived images of Venus shown earlier in perspective, here is an example of what the same technology can do when applied to the Earth itself. This image was obtained using a spaceborne radar imaging system carried on board the space shuttle *Endeavour*, on 14 April 1994. It shows a family of dormant volcanoes in the Andes of northern Ecuador, where the city of Otavalo shows up in pink and Lake Otavalo is a black pit inside the triangle formed by the three volcanic peaks. From the top left, reading clockwise, the volcanoes are called Mojanda, Imabura and Cusin. There are lava domes visible on the northern flank of Mojanda, and a lake partly fills the summit crater of this volcano. Mojanda last erupted about 3400 years ago, but the large volcano visible at the bottom of the picture, Cayambe, was active only 600 years ago. This kind of radar mapping can be used both to study the traces of past eruptions and to help predict future eruptions – if a later mission shows a change in the topography of a volcano, this could be a sign that magma is pushing up from below the crust, ready to burst forth once again.

The region shown in this image is about 50 km from top to bottom of the page, and north is towards the upper right; if you want to find the region in an atlas, it is centred at 0.1°N, 78.1°W. The colours have been assigned arbitrarily to provide technical information about the way the different surface features of the Earth reflect the radar signals.

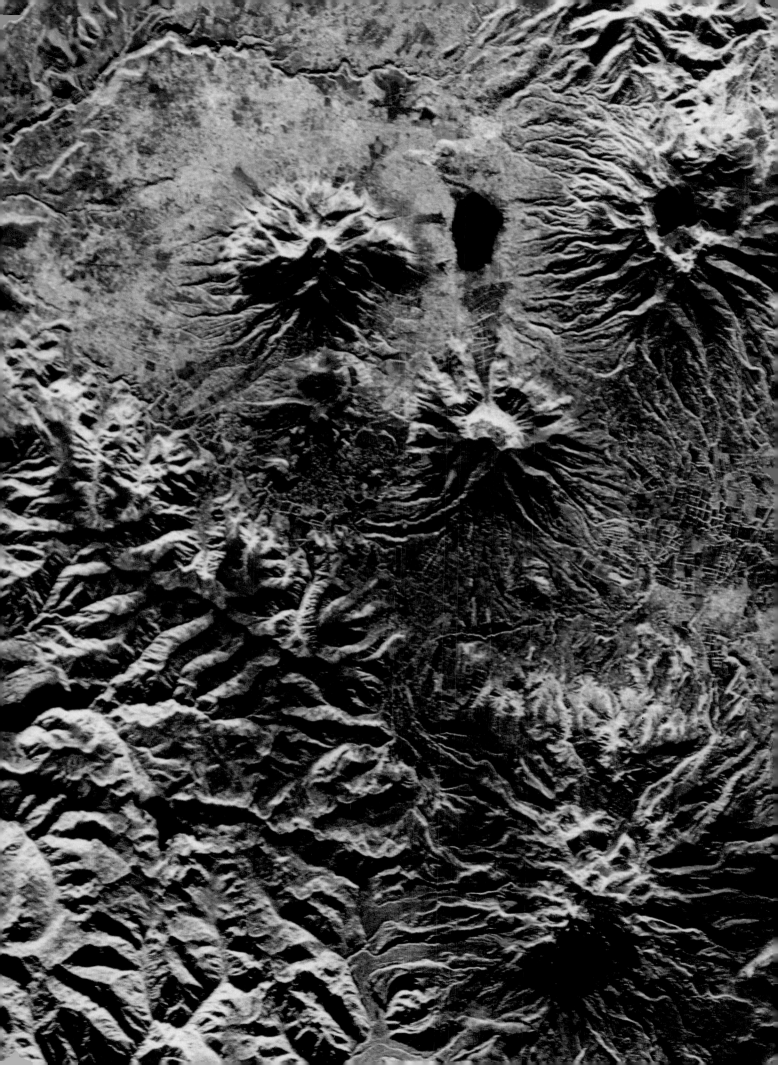

PLATE 18

LIFE ON EARTH II

A global view of the living planet floating in space (compare this with the 'projection' in Plate 16). Plant life in the oceans and on land reflects sunlight in a distinctive way, which can be picked out by the sensors on board satellites. Data from the satellites Nimbus-7 and NOAA-7 have been used to prepare this false-colour image in which areas of dense vegetation on land are coloured green, while the most abundant regions of microscopic plankton in the oceans are coloured red and yellow. Slightly confusingly, this means that yellow regions in the sea denote rich regions for life, whereas yellow regions on land indicate a relative sparsity of plant life. Apart from the beauty of the image, though, its importance is that it clearly shows how far the fertile region of the ocean extends up towards the north pole (the southern ocean is not visible in this picture). This kind of imaging makes it possible to monitor the effects on this essential part of the global food chain of changes in the climate, or of the depletion of ozone at high latitudes being caused by human activities.

PLATE 19

THE NOT-SO-PERFECT MOON

When Galileo Galilei first turned his telescope on the Moon in the first decade of the 17th century, he discovered that it is not a perfect sphere with dark and light coloured regions, but is marked by mountains and craters. This perceived imperfection of the Moon was regarded in some circles as heresy, since the Moon was thought to have been created by God, and dogma taught that it had to be a perfect sphere, as a mark of the perfection of God's work. Even in the face of the evidence of their own eyes, some theologians argued that the Moon must 'really' be encased in some invisible substance, like crystal, that did indeed form a perfect sphere, with the mountains and valleys embedded within the crystal. Galileo replied that he had no objection to this hypothesis, provided that he could hypothesise that there might be mountains and valleys of invisible crystal ten times larger than the mountains and valleys visible through his telescope!

This astonishingly crisp image, obtained (appropriately) by the Galileo spaceprobe on 7 December 1992, *en route* to Jupiter, shows the lumpiness of the Moon in striking detail, especially near the top of the image – the craters there, seen edge-on, look as if something has bitten pieces out of the Moon.

The image is particularly clear because the charge coupled device (CCD) detector carried by Galileo is sensitive not just to visible light, but in part of the infrared region of the spectrum, beyond the range visible to human eyes. Among other details that this highlights, the crater surrounded by bright rays of ejected material at the bottom of the image is the Tycho impact basin.

PLATE 20

MAN ON THE MOON

How could we resist it? The classic image of astronaut Edwin 'Buzz' Aldrin, photographed on the surface of the Moon on 20 July 1969, during the Apollo 11 mission. Astronaut Neil Armstrong, who took the picture, carefully set the shot up so that the faceplate of Aldrin's helmet reflects both Armstrong and the Lunar Module in which they had reached the surface. These were the first two human beings to set foot on the surface of the Earth's natural satellite; their footprints, visible on the dusty surface of the Moon, will stay there for thousands of years, because there is no wind to disturb them on the airless Moon.

While Aldrin and Armstrong were making history on the surface of the Moon, the Command Module pilot, Michael Collins, stayed in orbit around the Moon in the Apollo 11 vehicle, waiting for them to return.

PLATE 21

THE CRATER COPERNICUS

Galileo would have liked this one. The image was obtained by the Lunar Orbiter 5 spacecraft, in August 1967. It shows the edge of the crater Copernicus, a feature 93 km across that lies within the Mare Imbrium, the dark region of the Moon on the northern part of its visible face. The image shows the flat floor of the crater, a central mound, the crater rim and the rays of material which have sprayed out across its surroundings – the classic features of an impact crater.

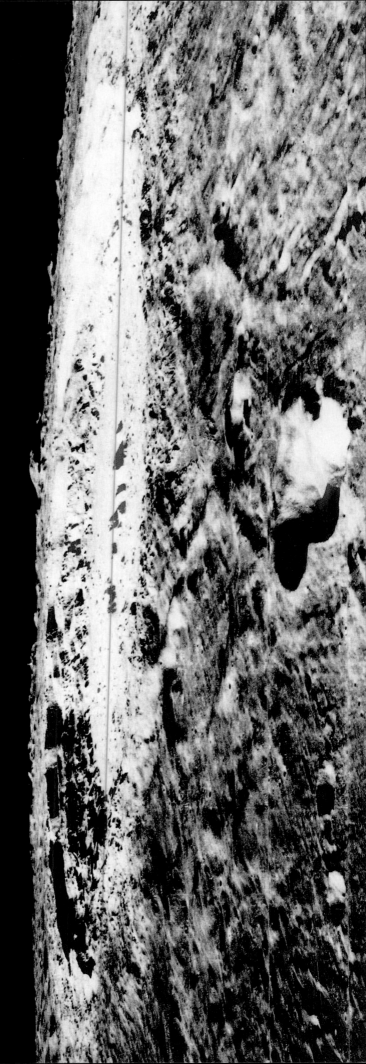

PLATE 22

MAKING THE MOST OF THE MOON

··

The power of modern technology in extracting the maximum amount of information from an image – or set of images – is illustrated in this 'picture' of the Moon, obtained by the Galileo spacecraft on 8 December 1992. At the time the images that went to make up this picture were taken, the probe was 425 000 km from the Moon (and 69 000 km from Earth). It took a series of fifteen separate images of the Moon, using three different filters which each allowed through one colour of light. Different kinds of material reflect different colours of light in different ways, so these images contain information about what the Moon is made of. The information from all these images was then combined to make a mosaic of very nearly the whole Moon (just part of the region at the bottom of the image is missing) and coloured, using the data from the different filters, to give an indication of the composition of the lunar surface material.

Different kinds of rock and dust show up as different colours in this image. Red regions largely correspond to the lunar highlands, while blue and orange colouring correspond to the lava flows of the low-lying mare, bluer mare containing lavas richer in titanium than orange mare. Mare Tranquillitatis is a deep blue patch to the right of the image, and Mare Serenitatis is the smaller, orange circular patch at the upper left of Mare Tranquillitatis. Small purple splotches are deposits produced by explosive volcanic eruptions long ago, and the distinctive crater at the bottom of the image, Tycho, is a feature 85 km across produced by a relatively recent impact.

Galileo actually followed a tortuous route to Jupiter, swinging past Venus once and the Earth twice in order to pick up speed, which is why pictures like this date from the early 1990s, even though the probe was launched in 1989 (*see also* page 12).

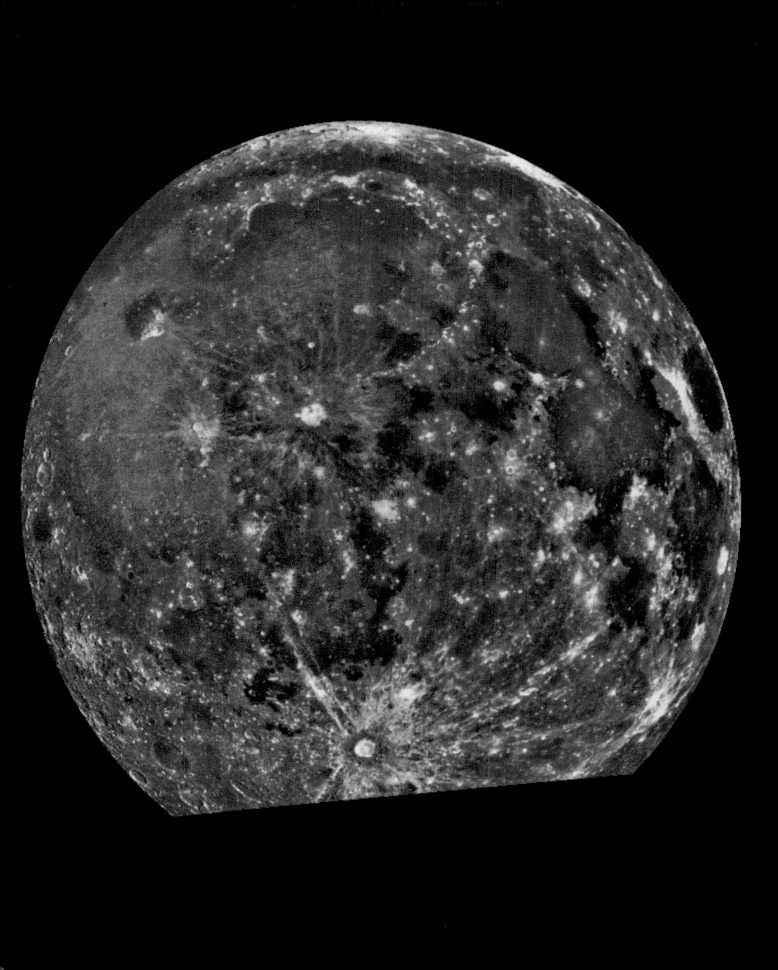

PLATE 23

THE RED PLANET

This is *not* a false colour image – Mars really is the Red Planet. Bigger than the Moon, it has enough gravitational pull to cling on to a thin trace of atmosphere. But because there is no life on Mars, and nothing like the kind of strong weathering that occurs in the thicker, wetter atmosphere of the Earth, the craters that scar its surface are much more easy to see than those on our home planet. The extent of this ancient cratering shows that the rain of debris that affected the inner planets when the Solar System was young extended all the way out to Mars, whose average distance from the Sun is 1.5 times the average distance of the Earth from the Sun. But, unlike Mercury and the Moon, Mars is also marked by the presence of a handful of huge volcanoes, each bigger than anything on Earth, as well as many smaller volcanic peaks. The largest, Olympus Mons, is 25 km high (three times taller than Mount Everest on Earth) and 600 km in diameter at its base. Because the flanks of the volcano are relatively free from craters, it must be a young feature, in geological terms, which was still erupting as recently as 100 million years ago, when dinosaurs roamed the Earth. Although Olympus Mons is a so-called shield volcano of the same type as the main island of Hawaii, it contains enough material to make a hundred full-size copies of that island.

Volcanic eruptions have changed the appearance of much of the northern hemisphere of Mars, which is also marked by what seem to be channels carved by running water when the planet was young and had a thicker atmosphere (we know these channels are very old, because there are many craters which cut across them). By contrast, the southern hemisphere of Mars is heavily cratered and, like the surfaces of Mercury and the Moon, seems to have changed little since the Solar System was young.

PLATE 24

THE FIRST MARTIAN EXPLORER

The tiny Sojourner rover vehicle (about the size of a shoebox) captured the imagination of millions of people when it became the first mobile explorer on the surface of Mars in 1997, as part of the Pathfinder mission. This was the first of a new style of planetary probe, summed up by the slogan 'faster, cheaper, better'. In the case of Pathfinder, 'cheaper' means about $150 million – which, NASA scientists like to point out, compares with the cost of making a blockbuster movie. The next Mars mission, Mars Global Surveyor, went into orbit around the red planet later in 1997, and after manouvering gradually into a close orbit around the planet should begin mapping its surface in detail in 1999.

In this image, taken by the cameras on board the Pathfinder lander which carried Sojourner to Mars, the little rover sits on top of Mermaid Dune, a region of dark material surrounded by brighter Martian surface. The tracks of the rover show as darker red in the foreground. Sojourner operated on the surface for three months (twelve times its design lifetime of seven days) and sent back 550 images; Pathfinder itself (now renamed Sagan Memorial Station, in honour of the late Carl Sagan) operated on the surface for the same period (it was designed to operate for one month) and sent back more than 16 000 images, as well as technical data about conditions on the surface of Mars.

PLATE 25

A MARTIAN PANORAMA

This is what Mars would look like if you had eyes in the back of your head, as well as the front. It is a full 360 degree panorama, obtained by the Pathfinder cameras over the course of three consecutive Martian days, in order to ensure the same lighting and shadow conditions for all regions of the surface visible. The Sojourner rover can be seen just to the right of the middle of the picture, nuzzled up against the rock called Yogi, so that its sensors can analyse the chemical composition of the rock. Turn the book sideways so that the pathfinder platform is at the bottom of the page; then, looking more or less towards Sojourner and Yogi, imagine the right and left edges of the image wrapped around in a circle to meet behind your head to get a feel for the all-round view from Pathfinder.

The tracks of Sojourner leading from the ramp by which it reached the surface from Pathfinder, and past the first rock it visited (known as Barnacle Bill) can also be seen.

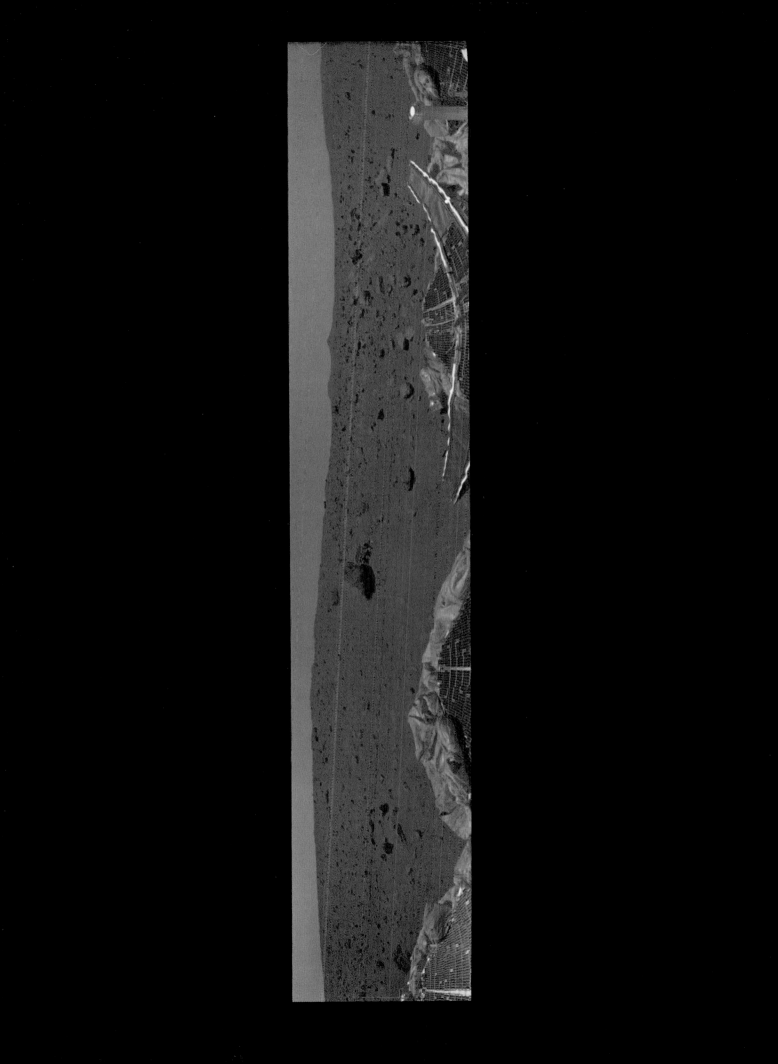

PLATE 26

GEOLOGICAL ACTIVITY ON MARS

Although it is now more than twenty years since the Viking probes visited Mars, the wealth of data they sent back to Earth is still providing food for thought. This image, released by NASA only in 1995, was obtained using the standard trick of looking at Mars (from Viking Orbiter cameras) through three different coloured filters, and combining data from the three images to give, in this case, a more or less true-colour view of a region centred on the feature known as Syria Planum. The region is marked by clear signs of geological activity, including volcanoes, and fractures and folds in the rocks caused by movement of the crust. Different regions show up in different colours because of the presence of different amounts of wind-blown sand, and probably because some of the rock itself has changed colour as it has weathered slowly over millions of years.

PLATE 27

A MOON OF MARS

Mars has two small moons, Phobos and Deimos. But these are not the same kind of object as our Moon, merely pieces of left-over cosmic rubble that have been captured into orbit around Mars, instead of slamming into its surface. As such, they are typical of the objects that caused the cratering we can still see on the surfaces of Mars and the other inner planets today – and in all probability, very similar to the object that smashed into the Earth 65 million years ago and brought an end to the era of the dinosaurs.

There are few pictures of the moons of Mars from close up, but in 1971 the Mariner 9 spaceprobe passed by Phobos and took this picture, from a distance of 2140 km. It is clear from this image that Phobos itself has been battered by many collisions with smaller objects during its lifetime. The orbit of Phobos is unstable, and slowly decaying; in about 30 million years from now it too will smash into the surface of Mars, adding a rather impressive crater to the markings on the surface of the Red Planet.

Phobos measures roughly 27 by 21 by 19 km, and orbits Mars once every 7 hours 40 minutes at a distance of 9380 km. Because this is faster than the rate at which Mars rotates (the length of one day on Mars is just 40 minutes longer than the length of one day on Earth), from the surface of Mars Phobos is seen to move backwards across the sky, rising in the west and setting in the east.

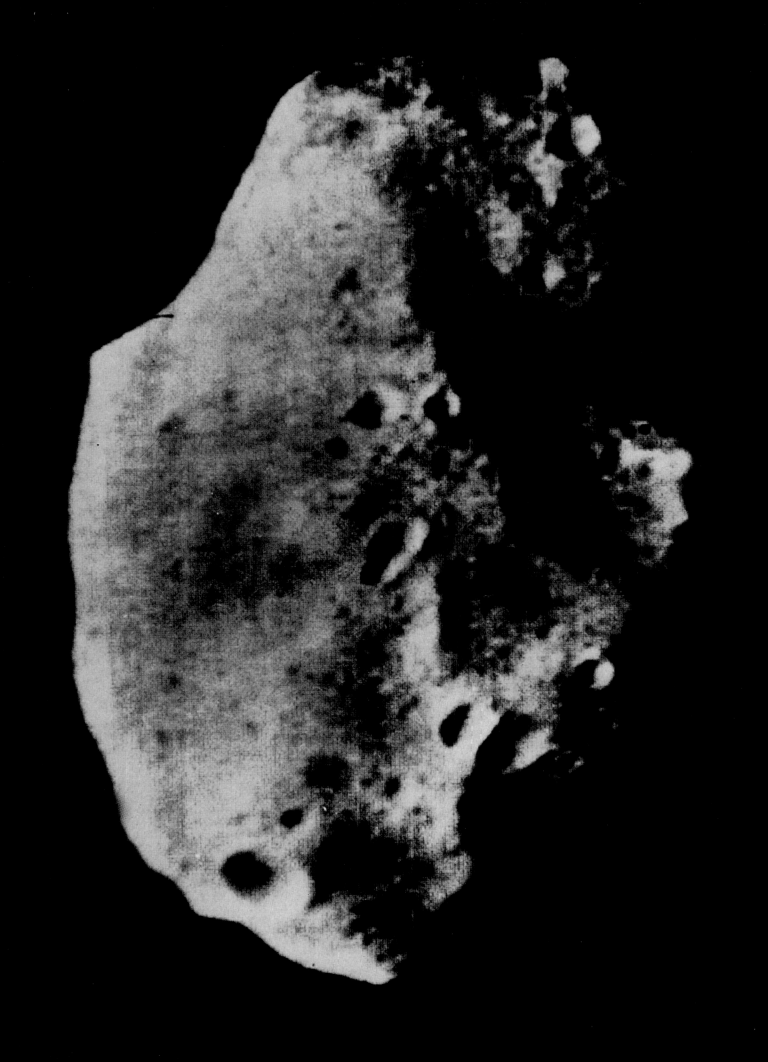

PLATE 28

ASTEROID GASPRA

....

Even a glance at this image of asteroid 951 Gaspra, obtained by the Galileo spacecraft on its way to Jupiter on 29 October 1991, shows that it bears a striking similarity to Phobos (Plate 27). Gaspra is a typical member of the belt of asteroids that lies between the orbits of Mars and Jupiter, and is also typical of the kind of cosmic rubble that pounded the inner planets when the Solar System was young. It is 19 by 12 by 11 km in size (slightly smaller than Phobos); the region illuminated by sunlight (shining from the left of the picture) in this image measures about 18 km from upper left to lower right.

This image is a masterpiece of data processing, produced using all the best data from Galileo. The basic image is a high-resolution black-and-white photograph of the asteroid, but colour information obtained by viewing the asteroid through three different filters in turn has been added as well. To the naked eye, the subtle variations in colour of the asteroid would not be noticeable; here, the contrast has been exaggerated slightly and false colour used to highlight the different regions of the surface of Gaspra. Blue areas are more reflective, and also show absorption of light at wavelengths typical of absorption by the mineral olivine, a semi-precious stone here on Earth. These regions tend to be along the ridges of Gaspra, and associated with some of the more sharply defined (and therefore, presumably, younger) craters. Slightly reddish regions are associated with relatively low-lying parts of the asteroid's surface, and are less reflective. The explanation for these differences is that underlying rock has been exposed in the bluer regions, while dusty debris has accumulated in the redder regions.

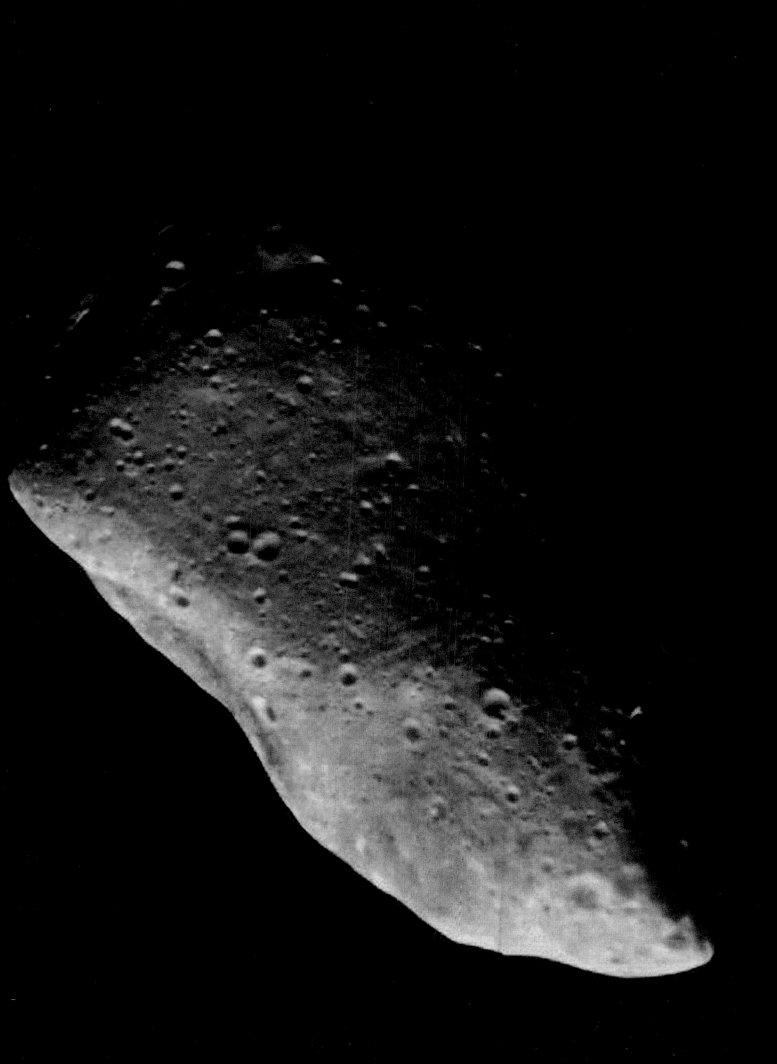

PLATE 29

A COMETARY STRING OF PEARLS

Although most comets orbit the Sun far away in the Oort Cloud, we become aware of them only when they fall in towards the Sun, crossing the orbit of Jupiter and getting hot enough to produce a glowing tail of gas that streams out behind them (*see* p. 25). The most spectacular of these visitors in recent times in astronomical terms (although it was never visible to the naked eye from Earth) was the comet discovered by Carolyn and Gene Shoemaker and David Levy in March 1993. Since it was the ninth comet discovered by the team, it is officially known as Shoemaker–Levy 9; but to everyone it is *the* Shoemaker–Levy comet. It passed by Jupiter so close that the icy ball of material at the nucleus of the comet was torn apart by the gravity of the giant planet into a 'string of pearls', twenty-one of which are visible in this picture, obtained by the Wide Field Planetary Camera on the Hubble Space Telescope. The length of the string of pearls pictured here is 1.1 million km, three times the distance from the Earth to the Moon. The largest of the cometary fragments in the string were between 2 and 4 km across. The whole string of cometary debris orbited Jupiter a few times, and then crashed into the planet in a series of spectacular impacts in July 1994.

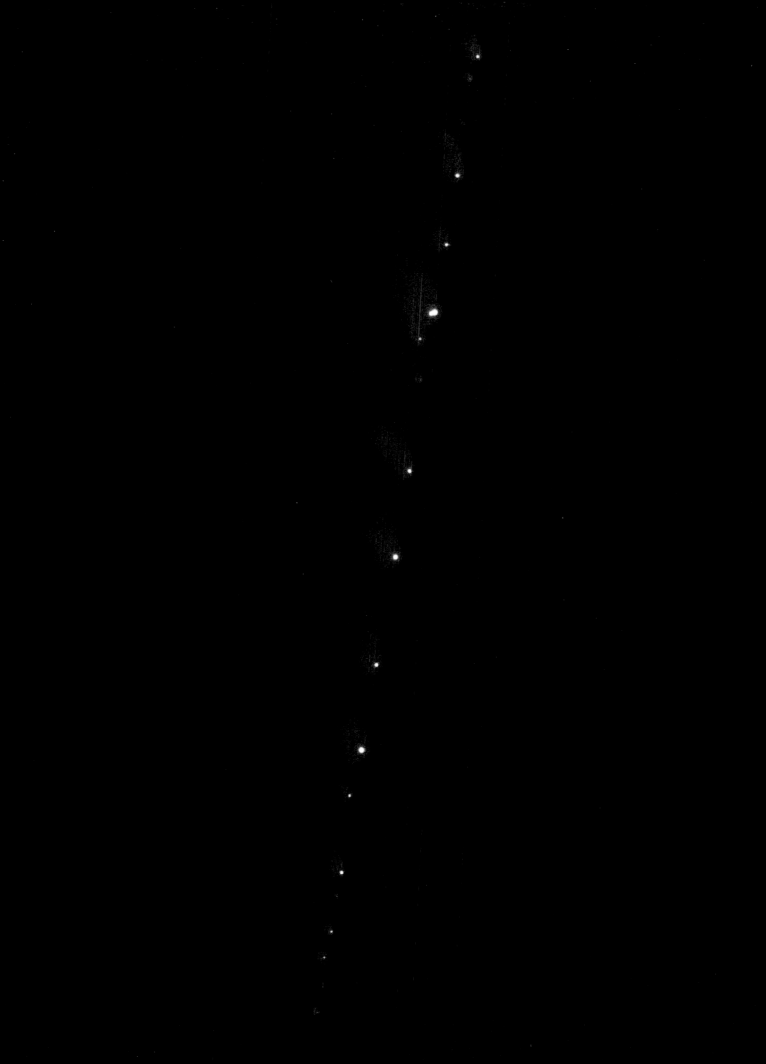

PLATE 30

THE HEART OF A COMET

The closest view of the heart of a comet yet obtained was captured by the spaceprobe Giotto, which flew past the nucleus of Halley's Comet in March 1986, during the most recent passage of the comet through the inner Solar System. Although the probe approached to within 596 km of the nucleus of the comet, sending back scientific data all the time, its cameras were knocked out by an impact with a small piece of cometary material soon after this picture was taken, from a distance of 6500 km, 95 seconds before closest approach.

The images and other data sent back show that, as expected, the nucleus is a lump of icy material, with 80 per cent of its mass in the form of water-ice. But most astronomers were surprised by observations which suggest that there are large lumps of rock embedded in the ice – not a flying snowball, but an icy rock pile. They were also surprised at how dark the surface is (the dark nucleus is just visible in the upper left of the picture; the bright stuff we see here is gas streaming out and away from the nucleus). The nucleus is an irregularly shaped object, roughly 16 by 8 by 8 km, about the size of the island of Manhattan. Its surface is literally blacker than coal, and reflects less than 4 per cent of the light that falls upon it. This makes the nucleus very hard to see, even with the best telescopes, and because they had assumed it must be more reflective than this, astronomers had calculated that the nucleus was smaller than Giotto revealed it to be. The black surface (which is rich in carbon compounds) is now explained as a crusty layer of dusty material that forms each time the comet passes close by the Sun (Halley's Comet comes in as close as 0.6 AU to the Sun, closer than Venus does). The heat of the Sun makes the comet active, and the gas jetting out from cracks in its surface (as we see in this image) carries dust with it. But when the comet is far away from the Sun at the other end of its orbit (which, in the case of Halley's Comet, is at 35 AU, beyond the orbit of Neptune), the black dust settles back down over the surface. It is very likely that other cometary nuclei are equally dark and unreflective, and that their sizes have been underestimated in the same way.

PLATE 31

THE GIANT PLANET

Jupiter is by far the largest planet in the Solar System, so large that the Earth would fit into Jupiter just over 1400 times. Jupiter actually contains 70 per cent of the mass of all the planets put together. Jupiter is the first of the gas giant planets, which are made up almost entirely of hydrogen and helium (as the Sun is) and do not have solid surfaces like the Earth and other terrestrial planets.

Such a massive planet dominates the Solar System and, it has been argued, helps to protect life on Earth. The planet acts as a giant cosmic vacuum cleaner, capturing many comets and asteroids before they enter the inner Solar System and preventing them from hitting Earth. One of these captures was seen recently as Comet Shoemaker–Levy collided with Jupiter.

Jupiter is thought to be the cause of the asteroid belt as well. Its powerful gravitational field is thought to have pulled and pushed rocks in the asteroid belt, preventing them from joining together and forming a planet. What we now see there is the remaining debris from a failed planet.

Jupiter is so large that it has its own mini 'solar system', in particular the four giant Galilean satellites (three of which are larger than the Moon) and twelve other known satellites, many of which are little more than captured asteroids. This picture from Voyager 1 shows the two most interesting Galilean moons – Io and Europa, about which we have much more to say – as they cross the face of Jupiter. Io (on the left) is passing by the Great Red Spot, a huge storm in Jupiter's atmosphere.

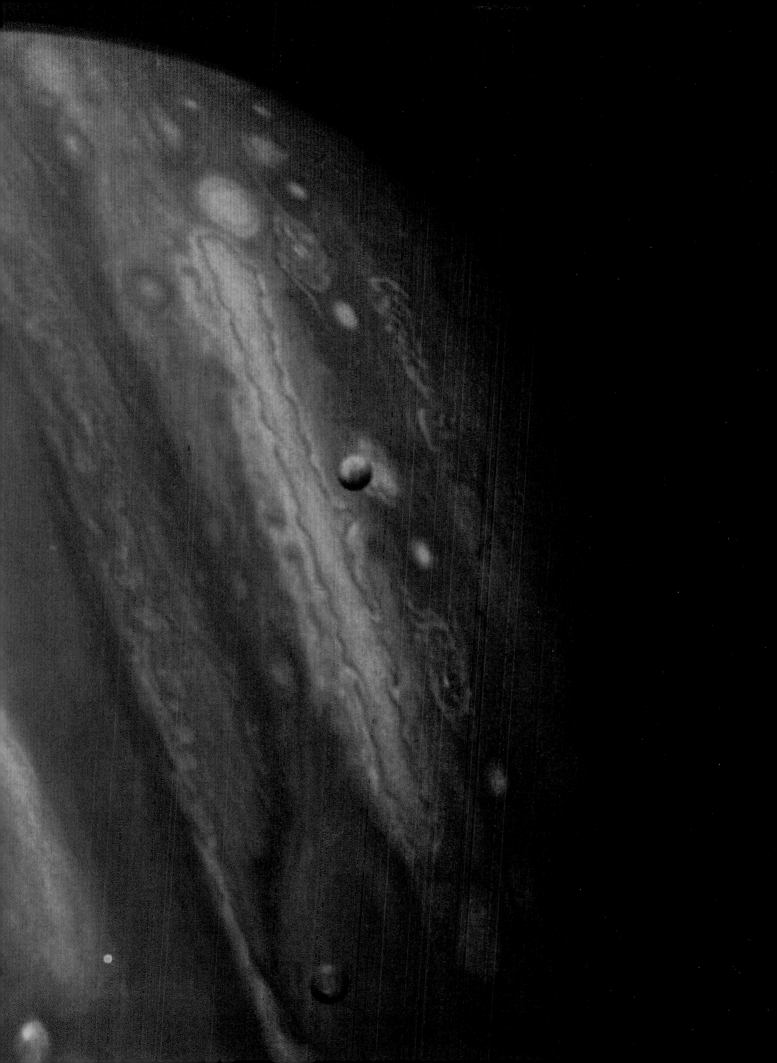

PLATE 32

TWO VIEWS OF EUROPA

....

This double image of one of the moons of Jupiter, Europa, provides a stunning example of the detail available in the pictures sent back to Earth by the Galileo probe. By showing the same image twice in slightly different fashions, we can also indicate the effects of the kind of false-colour treatment that is commonly used to highlight features of particular scientific interest.

If you turn the page so that the images are side by side, the view on the left is a close approximation to the natural colour of Europa, as it would appear to the unaided human eye. The image on the right is a colour-enhanced version which brings out even more clearly the differences between the different materials that make up the crust of the moon. Europa is essentially a smooth ball of ice (the smoothest object known in the Solar System), with rock embedded in it. The dark brown regions are rocky material, some of which may have come from within Europa, and some of which may have arrived in the form of asteroids crashing in to the moon. The bright plains in the polar regions at the top and bottom of the right-hand image are coded in shades of blue to distinguish regions of coarse-grained ice (dark blue) from regions covered by finer-grained ice (light blue). The incredibly fine lines, only 20–40 km wide, and running like veins through the ice, are fractures in the surface, some of them more than 3000 km long, like the fractures that might be produced by hitting a glass marble with a small hammer – but nobody is sure what caused them to form. Evidence that Europa does get struck blows from space can be seen in the lower right of the image, where there is a young impact crater about 50 km across. The most likely explanation for the lack of craters across most of the surface is that liquid water has seeped out from the interior and filled in the craters with ice, but the presence of some surface features suggests that at least part of the surface has been stable for at least 10 million years. Most of the surface is probably younger than that – possibly much younger (*see* the caption to Plate 34).

The image was obtained by Galileo on 7 September 1996, from a distance of 677 000 km (a little less than twice the distance from the Earth to the Moon). Europa is 3139 km in diameter, slightly smaller than our own Moon. It takes just over 3.5 days to orbit Jupiter.

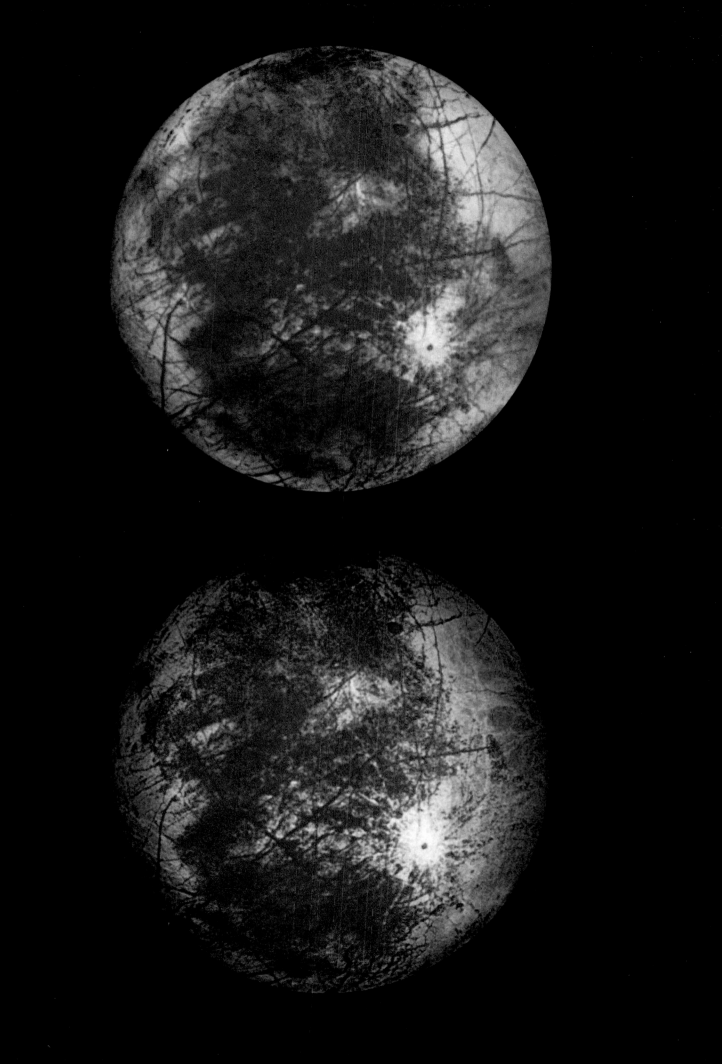

PLATE 33

EUROPA IN CLOSE-UP

This false-colour image shows a region of Europa known as Minos Linea in more detail. It was obtained by the Galileo spaceprobe on 28 June 1996. The area covered by this image is about 1260 km from top to bottom of the page, and the smallest features resolved by the imaging system on board Galileo are less than 2 km across. The vein-like cracks in the ice seem to be filled with material that has seeped into them from below the icy surface of the moon. Europa almost certainly has a rocky core below its ice-covered surface, with liquid water present at least part of the time in the boundary between them; it is probably heated in its interior by the tides raised in the solid rock by Jupiter, constantly flexing the core.

The visible surface is a cracked layer of ice lying on top of the liquid water, which is heated from below in a manner reminiscent of the way underwater volcanic activity on Earth warms the deep ocean. On Earth, the heat and chemicals from this volcanic activity have acted as a kind of geological incubator, giving rise to weird life forms that never see the Sun; it is just possible that something similar may exist in the depths of the oceans of Europa, far beneath the visible crust.

Close-up images obtained by the Galileo probe in April 1997 and December 1997 (*see* Plate 34) suggest that much of the icy surface is much younger and thinner than had previously been suspected; the images show icebergs and flat blocks of ice jostling together, just like the icy debris seen on the polar seas of the Earth during the spring thaw of the polar sea ice.

PLATE 34

EUROPA: EXTREME CLOSE-UP

The Galileo spaceprobe proved so durable and successful that after completing its two-year primary mission of exploration of the Jupiter system, it was sent on another tour of the Jovian moons, planned to last until 1999. One of the first objectives of this extended mission was to obtain an extreme close-up view of Europa on a close pass over the surface of the moon, which took place on 16 December 1997. This image was obtained during that flyby, at a distance of just 200 km above the frozen surface. It provides the clearest evidence yet that the visible surface of Europa is only an icy crust covering an ocean of liquid water. There are now plans to send a submersible probe to Europa some time in the early 21st century, to penetrate the ice and search for signs of life in the ocean below.

By the end of 1997, Galileo had sent back a gigabyte of data and 1800 images, including hundreds of close-up pictures of Jupiter's moons, to Earth; it was planned to fly by Europa another seven times, as well as revisiting Callisto and Io.

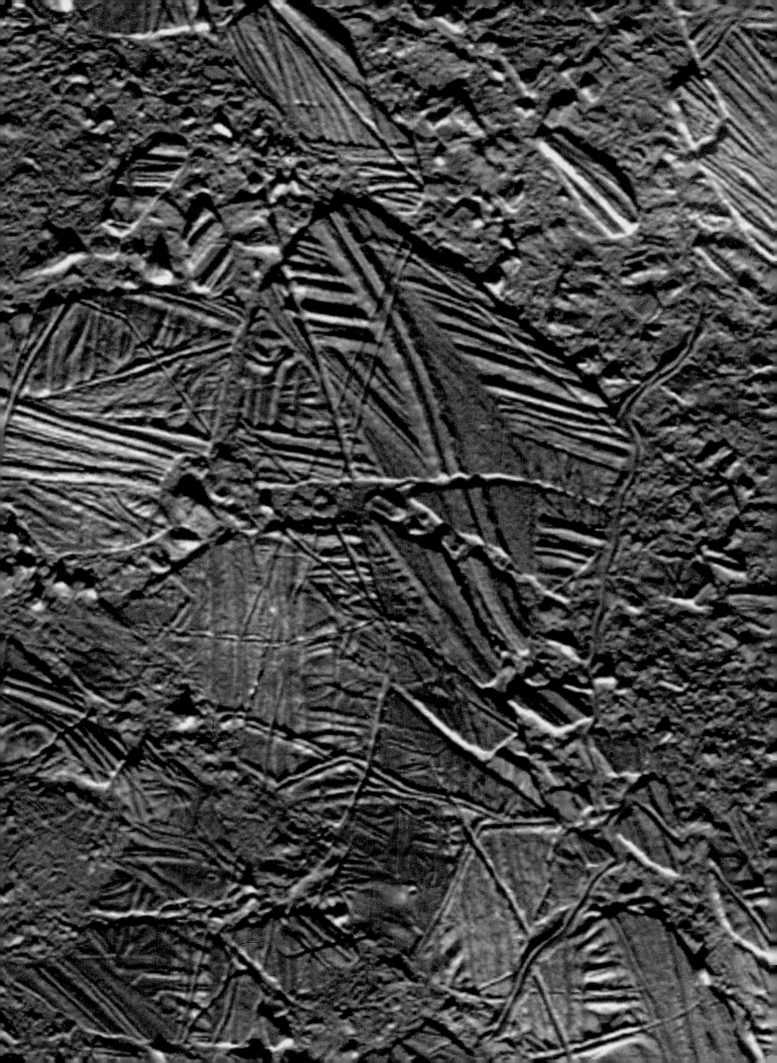

PLATE 35

IO, THE VOLCANIC MOON

In the whole of the story of the exploration of the Solar System to date, perhaps the biggest surprise came when the Voyager probes found active volcanoes on Io, the innermost of the four large moons that orbit Jupiter. It is now clear that Io is the most volcanically active body in the entire Solar System. It orbits so close to Jupiter (at a distance of only 422 000 km, almost as close as the Moon is to Earth) that the tidal pull of the giant planet squeezes the moon rhythmically, generating heat in its interior. It is this internal heat that drives the volcanic activity. The material spewed out from the interior of the moon by this activity is rich in sodium, which forms a cloud around the moon; but the spectacular coloration of the surface shown here is caused by the presence of sulphur and sulphur compounds laid down on the surface by the volcanism.

This image, from the Galileo spaceprobe, was obtained by adding colour data obtained through three different filters on 7 September 1996 to a high-resolution black-and-white image obtained on 6 November 1996. The colours are essentially natural, but have been slightly enhanced to emphasise the contrast between different regions of the surface. The colour data were obtained when the spaceprobe was 487 000 km from Io, and the high-resolution data from a series of pictures taken at distances ranging from 245 719 km to 403 100 km. The smallest features visible in this combined image are about 2.5 km across. Among the many striking details in this picture, just to the right of the centre a volcano is pouring out a black trail of ejected material, while just below this another volcano has spewed reddish sulphurous material out across the surface.

Io has a diameter of 3630 km (comparable to our Moon's 3476 km) and a mass 20 per cent greater than that of our Moon, showing that it is composed largely of rock. Like our Moon, it is locked in an orbit with one side always facing towards its parent planet; this view is of the side that is always turned away from Jupiter.

PLATE 36

THE OTHER GALILEAN SATELLITES

As well as the imperfections on the surface of the Moon, one of the first discoveries made by Galileo when he turned his telescope towards the heavens at the beginning of the 17th century was that Jupiter is circled by four large moons. These are now known as the Galilean satellites of Jupiter. The image of Jupiter circled by its moons was instrumental in helping to establish the idea that the planets, including the Earth, circle the Sun in the same way; the Jovian system was, and is, perceived as a kind of miniature solar system. It is now known that Jupiter has a family of at least 16 moons (as well as a faint ring system), making the resemblance to the Solar System even more striking. But the four Galilean satellites are by far the biggest and most important of these – some of the lesser moons, like the two moons of Mars, are probably simply captured pieces of cosmic junk.

We have already looked at two of the Galilean satellites, Europa and Io. Here are the other two. Rotate the page clockwise through 90 degrees and Ganymede is on the left, with Callisto on the right. In order of their distances from Jupiter, Io is closest, followed by Europa, Ganymede and Callisto. Ganymede is the largest (indeed, the largest moon in the Solar System, and bigger than Mercury), with a diameter of 5262 km; it has a very low density, less than twice that of water, and is mainly made of ice. Callisto has a similarly low density, and is also largely made of ice, and is a little smaller than Ganymede, with a diameter of 4800 km (almost exactly the same size as Mercury). The two moons shown here are less active than the two inner Galilean satellites, because they are further from Jupiter and subjected to lower tidal stresses.

However, there has been some internal activity on Ganymede, which has partially resurfaced the moon since it formed. Callisto, even further from Jupiter, shows no sign of internal activity, and seems to have retained its primordial surface, which is now completely smothered by craters caused by impacts long ago. This, and other evidence, suggests that the Galilean moons formed in orbit around Jupiter from a disk of primordial material, in much the same way that the planets formed in orbit around the Sun.

PLATE 37

THE GREAT RED SPOT

No picture sequence of the Jovian system would be complete without a close-up of the Great Red Spot. The spot is essentially a huge weather system in the atmosphere of Jupiter, equivalent to the high-pressure systems (anticyclones) that drift across the surface of the Earth. But this anticyclone is three times the size of the entire Earth, and the winds around it have been blowing for at least three centuries – it was first observed by Robert Hooke, in 1664.

    This image was obtained by the spaceprobe Voyager 2, on 6 July 1979, from a range of 2 633 003 km.

PLATE 38

THE RINGS OF SATURN

Although Galileo, with the aid of his astronomical telescope, could see that there was something peculiar about the planet Saturn, which seemed to have a bulge on either side, it was only in the late 1650s that the Dutch astronomer Christiaan Huygens, using an improved telescope that he built with his brother Constantijn, discovered that Saturn is surrounded by a thin, flat ring, with a clear gap between the ring and the planet. Later observations, by Giovanni Cassini in 1675, showed that there is a gap in the rings, still known as the Cassini Division. But the true nature of the rings was not understood until 1859, when the Scottish physicist James Clerk Maxwell, in one of his earliest scientific papers, proved that the rings could not be solid objects, because if they were they would be torn apart by tidal forces; they must be made up of a myriad of tiny particles, each one in its own orbit around Saturn, like a tiny moon.

The fine structure of the rings is clearly brought out in images like this one, obtained by the spaceprobe Voyager 1 on 13 November 1980, looking back at Saturn from a distance of 1 500 000 km beyond the ringed planet on its journey out of the Solar System. The image was exposed to bring out the detail in the rings. The appearance of the ring system is reminiscent of the grooves in a vinyl record, but each groove is made up of many tiny moonlets following essentially the same orbit around Saturn.

It was Maxwell who invented the technique of making colour images by using information from three black-and-white photographs taken through three different coloured filters. Images like this one, obtained using the photographic technique invented by Maxwell, confirm the structure of the rings predicted by Maxwell more than a hundred years earlier.

PLATE 39

THE RINGED PLANET

This enhanced colour image of Saturn shows the distinctly flattened shape of the ringed planet. Saturn is nearly ten times bigger across than the Earth, and has a diameter of 120 660 km at its equator (it is the second largest planet in the Solar System, after Jupiter), but it spins so rapidly (the day on Saturn lasts just 10 hours 14 minutes) that centrifugal force makes it bulge at the equator so much that it is 10 per cent smaller measured pole to pole. The outermost part of the ring system visible here has a diameter of 272 400 km – but the rings are only about 100 m thick, incredibly thin in proportion to their diameter. The two main rings, picked out by Cassini more than 300 years ago, are known as the A ring (on the outside) and the B ring (the inner ring), separated by the Cassini Division, a gap 3 500 km across, almost as wide as the United States measured from the Pacific to the Atlantic coasts.

This image was obtained by one of the Voyager craft, but the record of which of the two Voyager probes it was, the exact date and the distance of the probe from Saturn have been lost in the NASA archive. Three of the moons of Saturn (Tethys, Dione and Rhea) can be seen against the black backdrop of space, and a fourth, Mimas, is visible passing in front of Saturn, on the left-hand side of the image just below the rings. Saturn has at least twenty moons, with more still being discovered (not counting the huge number of tiny moonlets that make up the rings).

PLATE 40

A BLACK-AND-WHITE-MOON

....

The moons of Saturn are as distinctive and strange as the moons of Jupiter. When investigated by spaceprobes for the first time, as for the moons of Jupiter they turned out to be nothing like the way astronomers had imagined them on the basis of the limited information available from ground-based telescopes. Iapetus, pictured here, is the outermost large moon of Saturn, and one of the most peculiar objects in the Solar System. It orbits Saturn once every 79 days at an average distance of 3 560 000 km (far outside the ring system), and has a diameter of 1600 km. Nothing very peculiar about that; but one side of the moon (the hemisphere that leads in the direction of the moon's orbital motion around Saturn) is a dark black colour, as if it were covered by material like tar or asphalt. It reflects so little light that the cameras on board Voyager 2 could pick out no details of the terrain. The other side of Iapetus, shown here, is brightly reflective and seems to be made of dirty ice and snow, with many large impact craters scarring its surface. Nobody knows why the two hemispheres should be so different.

This image was obtained on 22 August 1981, by Voyager 2. The smallest features visible are about 15 km across; no finer details are visible because Voyager 2 never went closer to Iapetus than about a million kilometres (more than twice the distance from the Earth to the Moon). This enigmatic moon is one of the primary targets for the Cassini mission, due to arrive at the Saturn system in 2004.

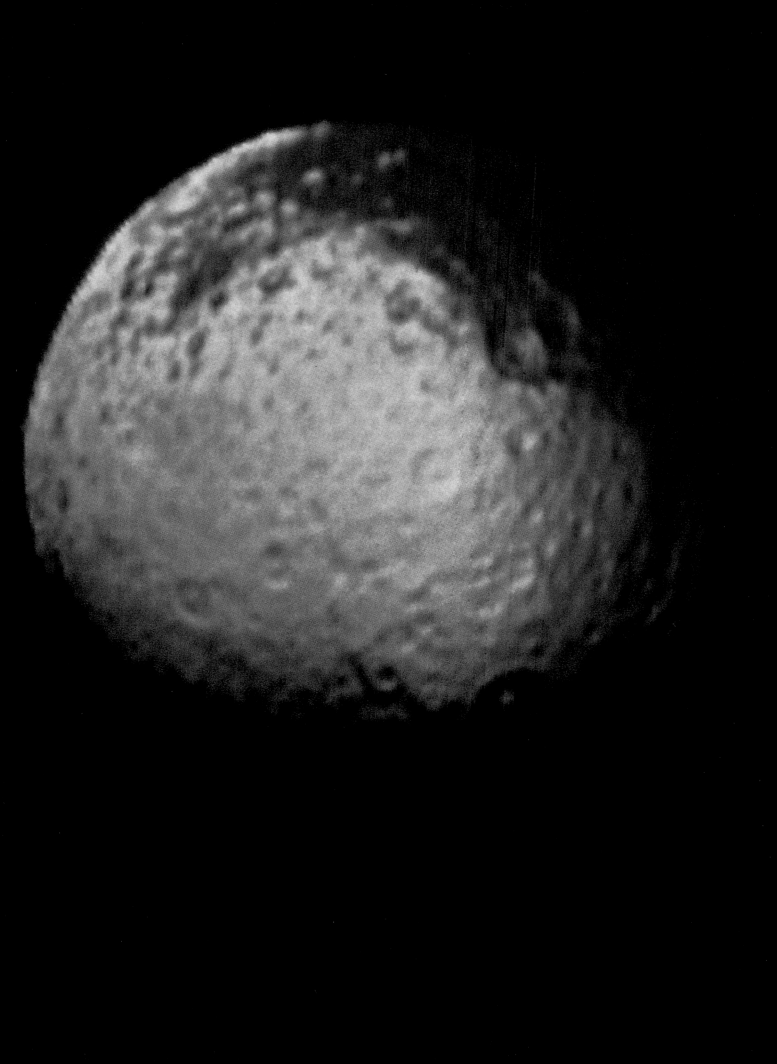

PLATE 41

ANOTHER HOME FOR LIFE?

At first sight, this is the least exciting image in the book. But it shows us one of the most interesting and potentially exciting places in the Solar System: Titan, the most likely place to find life outside the Earth. Titan, the largest moon of Saturn, orbits its parent planet at a distance of 1 222 000 km, once every 15 days. It has a diameter of 5150 km and a thick atmosphere (so thick that the pressure at the surface is one and a half times the pressure of the air at the surface of the Earth), mainly composed of nitrogen but laced with methane and ammonia, and shrouded (as shown in this image) by orange clouds which contain complex organic molecules produced by the activity of lightning in the chemical soup of the atmosphere. Don't be fooled by the word 'organic', though; to a chemist, organic molecules are complex compounds containing carbon. They are indeed important to life forms like ourselves, which are carbon-based, but they are not on their own proof of the existence of life. Nevertheless, it is thought that very similar conditions to those that exist on Titan today (nitrogen, methane, ammonia and the effects of lightning) existed on the Earth when the Solar System was young, and may have led to the emergence of living molecules.

On Earth, there were oceans of liquid water in which the complex chemistry of life could emerge. Titan, much farther from the Sun, is a frozen moon, with a surface temperature of minus 180 degrees Celsius, and all its water locked up in ice, so the complex molecules that may be the precursors of life remain as an orange haze in the atmosphere. Radar pulses bounced off Titan in the late 1980s suggest that there may be a partially liquid surface, perhaps a slushy ocean of liquid methane and frozen water.

In a few billions of years from now, when the Sun nears the end of its life, it will swell up to become what is known as a red giant star. The extra heat from the ageing star will incinerate the inner planets of the Solar System, but may bring Titan to life, as it emerges from deep freeze and perhaps passes through the same sequence of events that led to the emergence of life on Earth. In the much closer future, investigations of Titan may provide information about what the Earth was like when it was young, and how life got started in our home planet. The next step in this investigation will come when the Cassini craft drops a small probe, known as Huygens, into the atmosphere of Titan.

PLATE 42

ANOTHER BATTERED MOON

Totally unlike either Iapetus or Titan, Tethys, another of the moons of Saturn, shows a battered face reminiscent of the cratering that scars the surface of Mercury – another example of the similarity between the way in which the larger moons formed in orbit around the giant planets and the way in which the planets themselves formed in orbit around the Sun. This image, obtained by Voyager 2, clearly shows a particularly large (and relatively recent) impact crater in the upper right, near a wide trench that stretches diagonally across the ice-covered surface of the moon. Tethys orbits Saturn once every 45 hours, at a distance of 294 670 km. It has a diameter of 1060 km.

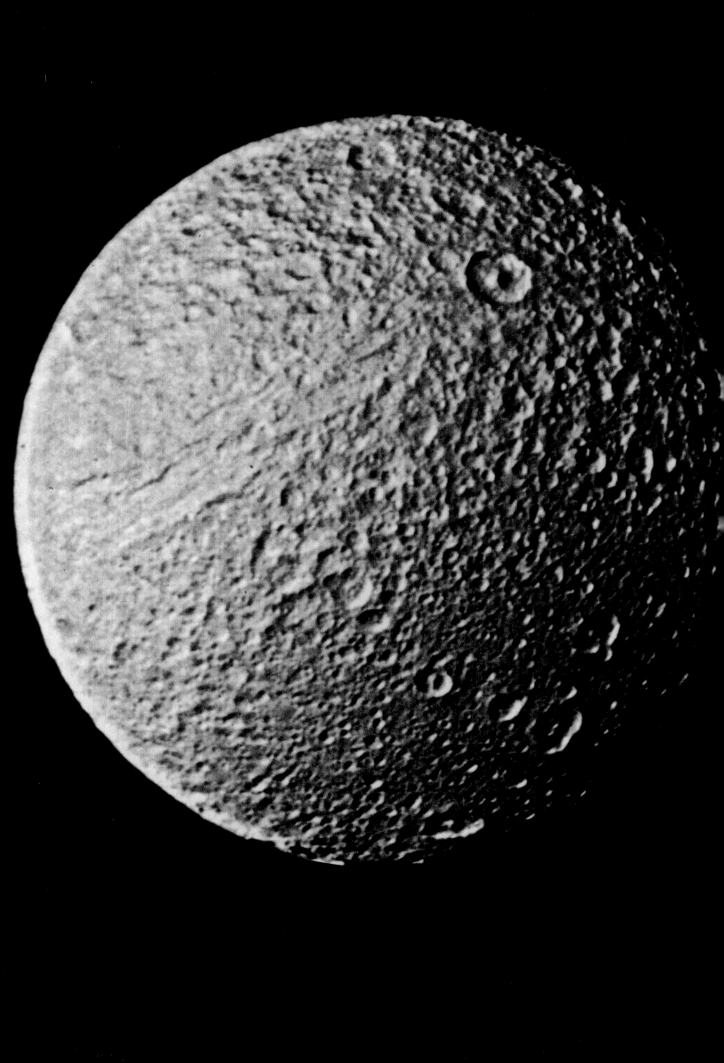

PLATE 43

THE CLOUDS OF SATURN

Whereas the image in Plate 38 was exposed to bring out detail in the rings of Saturn, the rings are scarcely visible in this image, which has been processed to emphasise the coloured bands and other features formed in the clouds of Saturn itself. As well as the coloured bands, you can see spots which are thought to be similar to (but much bigger than) thunderstorms on Earth. The image makes no pretence of representing the true colours of Saturn – the violet-coloured belt of clouds would actually look brown to the human eye – but it is a spectacular image of a fascinating planet.

The picture is based on data obtained by Voyager 1 on 18 October 1980, using three different coloured filters. The edge of the ring system at the lower right has been clipped off by the cameras on board Voyager 1, which were not quite perfectly centred on Saturn.

PLATE 44

SATURN: A FAMILY PORTRAIT

···

This family portrait of the Saturnian system was put together by the Voyager project team using images obtained by Voyager 1 during November 1980. The montage shows the moon Dione in the foreground, Saturn and its rings behind Dione, the moons Tethys and Mimas in the distance to the upper right, Enceladus and Rhea at the lower left, and orange Titan far away at the top. This is like an artist's impression, of course; you could never see the Saturnian system looking just like this in real life, though every image is a genuine Voyager 1 photograph.

PLATE 45

URANUS: A FAMILY PORTRAIT

In 1986, the Voyager spacecraft found ten previously unknown moons of Uranus, and in 1997 two more small moons, orbiting a long way out from the planet, were discovered by astronomers using the ground-based Hale Telescope on Mount Palomar. This brought the total number of Uranian moons known at the end of 1997 to seventeen. The 'new' moons had not been named at the time this book was written. One is 160 km across and the other just 80 km in diameter; they orbit at about 8 million km and 6 million km, respectively, from Uranus.

Uranus itself is visually one of the most boring objects in the Solar System – a featureless blue sphere. This image is a montage put together by NASA's Jet Propulsion Laboratory from two images obtained by Voyager 2, with the thin line of the Uranian ring system added by an artist. It shows the view of the giant planet as it might appear rising over the horizon of its moon Miranda.

PLATE 46

MIRANDA: A MYSTERIOUS MOON

The smallest (just under 500 km across) and innermost of the five largest moons of Uranus, Miranda has a geologically complex surface which seems to have resulted from the moon being smashed apart by a major impact, and the pieces then gradually drifting back together under the pull of their own gravity. The process may even have happened more than once. One result of this turbulent history is that the most striking feature on the surface of Miranda is a fault valley 15 km deep, which gives the jagged edge to the bottom right of the moon's surface in this Voyager 2 image. This bizarre history of the moon may be related to the bizarre nature of the Uranian system as a whole. Unlike the other planets in the Solar System, which orbit upright as they circle around the Sun, Uranus orbits on its side, with first one pole and then the other pointing towards the Sun as it follows its own 84-year orbit. Uranus's moons and rings follow circular orbits around the equator of the planet, making the whole system like a bull's-eye target at right angles to the plane in which all the planets (including Uranus) orbit the Sun. It may be that this is the result of a massive impact by some object with Uranus long ago, which literally knocked the planet on its side and created the present system of moons around Uranus from the resulting debris.

Because the moons were spread out in this bull's-eye pattern at right angles to the trajectory of Voyager 2, the probe was able to make a close pass by only one moon as it passed through the system, and it just happened that Miranda was the one most easily targeted at the time, in January 1986. This image was produced by combining information from several of the individual images obtained by Voyager 2 during its flyby.

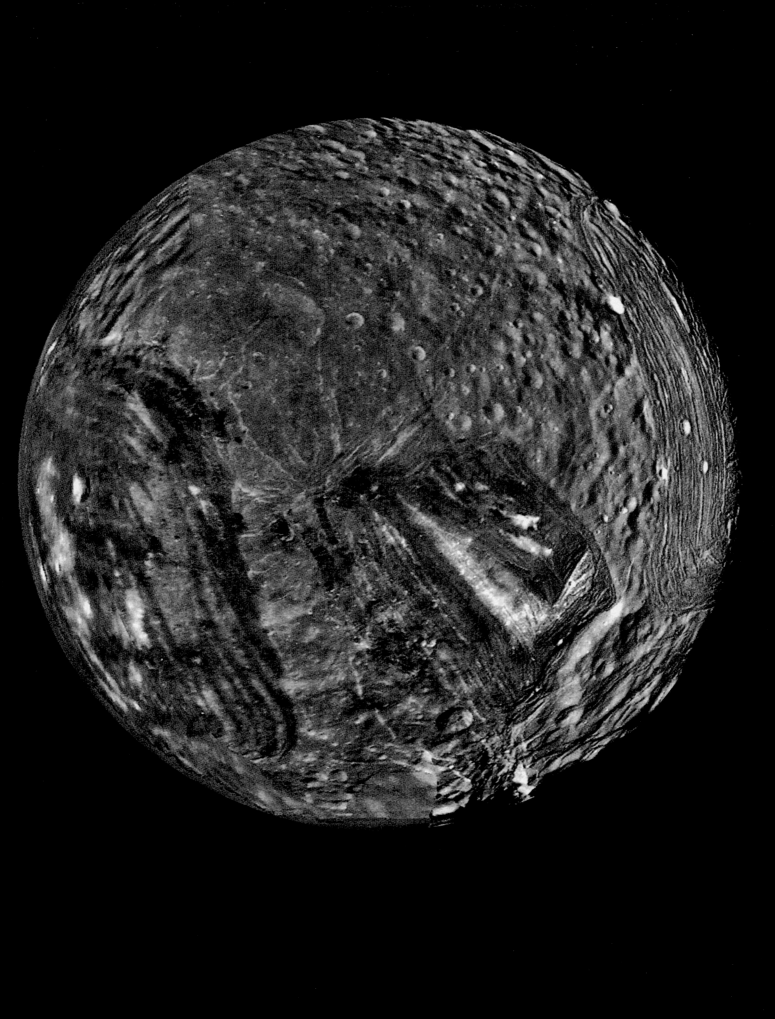

PLATE 47
INTO THE BLUE: NEPTUNE

During 16 and 17 August 1989, Voyager 2 took a series of pictures of Neptune. This picture, taken from that sequence, shows two distinctive features in the clouds of Neptune. The dark oval-shaped feature on the left (the Great Dark Spot, shown in more detail in Plate 48) travelled around Neptune once every 18.3 hours during this period of observation. The second dark spot, at the lower right of the image, travelled around the planet in 16.1 hours. The image is not quite true colour, because it has been processed to enhance the visibility of small features, but Neptune really would look blue and largely featureless to the human eye.

   The upper clouds of Neptune are actually made of methane, but there is a largely transparent and haze-free atmosphere above the clouds, unlike on Uranus. The deep blue colour is caused by the scattering of sunlight in the atmosphere – the same process that makes the sky look blue from the surface of the Earth. The day on Neptune lasts for 16 hours and 7 minutes. As well as a family of at least eight moons it has four faint rings.

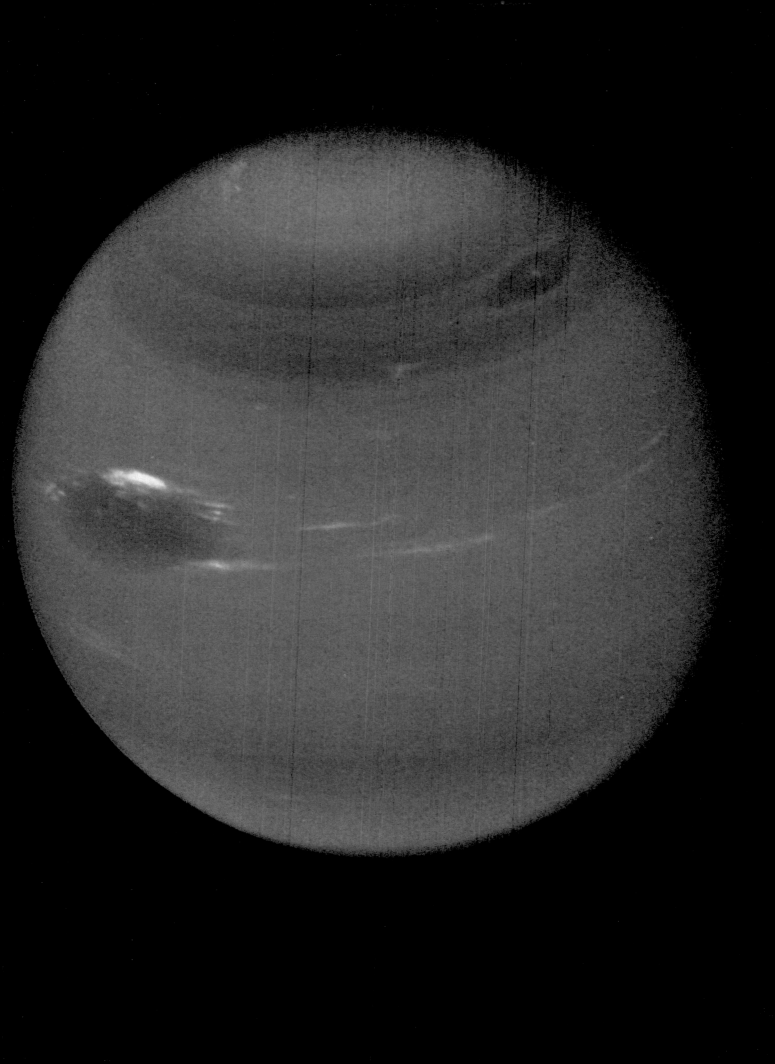

PLATE 48

THE GREAT DARK SPOT

This Voyager 2 image of part of the surface of Neptune was obtained from a distance of 2.8 million km, and shows the Great Dark Spot in more detail. Surrounding the Spot are white clouds that rotate with it and change their structure rapidly. All these features were moving from west to east at different speeds during the period when Voyager 2 observed Neptune, in August 1989, and were clearly being carried by strong winds in the planet's atmosphere.

The Great Dark Spot was about 6000 km across and 10 000 km long; the Earth would fit neatly inside it. It rotated anticlockwise, once every 16 days, and sat at almost exactly the same latitude on Neptune (20°S) as the Great Red Spot (*see* Plate 37) does on Jupiter. Both Great Spots were of similar shape and comparable in size in proportion to the diameter of their host planets. Since the exact origin of these spots is not known, nobody knows whether this is just a coincidence, or a profound feature of the structure of the giant planets. But the Great Dark Spot was not as long-lived as its Jovian counterpart: observations made by the Hubble Space Telescope in 1994 showed that it had disappeared.

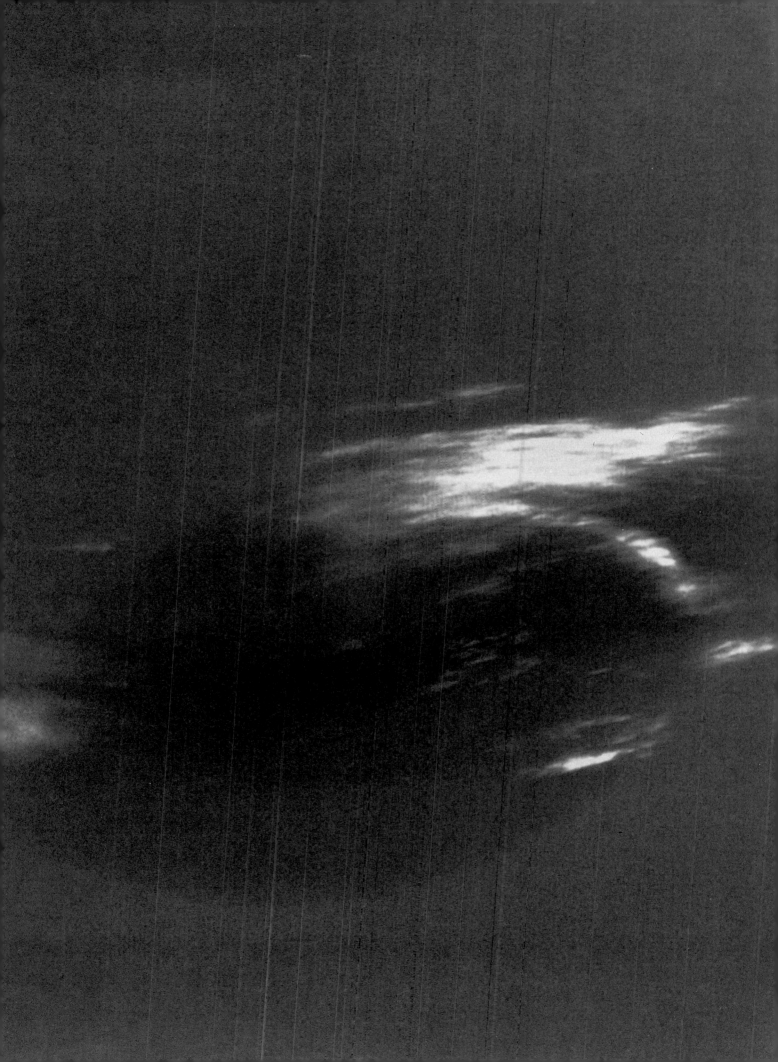

PLATE 49

PLUTO AND CHARON

No spaceprobe has yet visited Pluto, the most remote object in the Solar System usually dignified with the name 'planet'. This picture of Pluto and its moon (or binary companion) Charon was taken by the Hubble Space Telescope on 21 February 1995. In fact, at that time Pluto was closer to the Sun than Neptune was; the highly eccentric orbit of the Pluto–Charon system takes it within Neptune's orbit for long stretches of time, including the interval from 1979 to 1999. When this photograph was taken Pluto was only 4.4 billion km (about 30 AU) from Earth, as close as it ever gets to us. This was one of the first pictures ever to show Pluto and Charon as separate, distinct disks, and it was by using images like this that astronomers determined the diameter of Pluto as 2302 km and that of Charon as 1186 km; the pair are separated by a distance of only 19 600 km. The temperature at the surface of Pluto is minus 223 degrees Celsius.

PLATE 50

THE PLUTO MAP

Pluto is two-thirds the size of the Earth's Moon, but 1200 times farther away. This makes these superficially unspectacular images among the most impressive achievements of observational astronomy. During late June and early July 1994, the Hubble Space Telescope took a series of photographs of Pluto as it rotated through one complete 6.4-day period. Each square picture element (pixel) in the Hubble images covers a square more than 160 km on a side on Pluto, so no feature smaller than that can be distinguished in the images. But after computer processing to clean up the pictures, astronomers have obtained the images shown here, which are maps of two opposite hemispheres of Pluto (so together they cover the entire surface of the ninth planet).

There are about a dozen main regions visible on the face of Pluto that can be distinguished, which means that it shows more large-scale contrast in its surface features than any other planet except Earth. Some of these features may be topographic structures, such as large impact craters or basins like the lunar maria. The most likely explanation of most of the pattern of bright and dark regions on the surface of Pluto, though, is that it is covered by different kinds of frost, which reflect sunlight in different degrees. In that case, these may be temporary features that migrate with the seasons. The prominent 'north polar cap' is almost certainly a seasonal feature of this kind – but since one year for Pluto lasts for 248 of our years, even seasonal features may last for a relatively long time.

And that (since we have already shown you images of comets in Plates 29 and 30) brings us to the end of our pictorial tour of the Solar System. But this is far from being the end of the story of the exploration of the Empire of the Sun, with both Cassini and a whole range of 'faster, cheaper, better' spaceprobes that will be sending back more spectacular images of the planets and moons of the Solar System as we move in to the 21st century.

APPENDIX 1: PRINCIPAL PLANETARY MISSIONS, 1973–97

YEAR	MONTH	ARRIVAL AT	COMMENTS
1973	November	—	Mariner 10 launched
1974	March	Mercury	Mariner 10's first encounter with Mercury (two more in September 1974 and March 1975)
1975	August	—	Viking 1 launched
	September	—	Viking 2 launched
1976	June	Mars	Viking 1 arrives, lander touches down on 20 July 1976
	August	Mars	Viking 2 arrives, lander touches down on 3 September 1976
1977	August	—	Voyager 2 launched
	September	—	Voyager 1 launched
1979	March	Jupiter	Voyager 1 passes through Jovian system
	July	Jupiter	Voyager 2 passes through Jovian system
1980	November	Saturn	Voyager 1 passes through Saturnian system
1981	August	Saturn	Voyager 2 passes through Saturnian system
	October	—	Venera 13 orbiter and lander launched
	November	—	Venera 14 orbiter and lander launched
1982	March	Venus	Veneras 13 and 14 land (they survive for 127 and 57 minutes, respectively)
1985	July	—	Giotto probe launched
1986	January	Uranus	Voyager 2 passes by Uranus
	March	Halley's Comet	Giotto encounters Halley's Comet
1989	May	—	Magellan orbiter launched from Space Shuttle
	August	Neptune	Voyager 2 passes Neptune
	October	Jupiter	Galileo probe launched from Space Shuttle
1990	August	Venus	Magellan arrives at Venus and functions until October 1994
1992	July	Comet	Giotto encounters its second comet: Grigg–Skjellerup
1994	January	Moon	Clementine launched, passes by the Moon several times
1995	December	Jupiter	Galileo arrives and its probe enters the Jovian atmosphere (Galileo is still operational)
		Sun	SOHO solar observatory launched (still operational)
1996	February	—	Near Earth Asteroid Rendezvous (NEAR) launched
	November	—	Mars Global Surveyor launched
	December	—	Mars Pathfinder launched
1997	June	Mathilde	NEAR passes close to asteroid Mathilde
	July	Mars	Mars Pathfinder lands, functions for 2 months
	September	Mars	Mars Global Surveyor enters Mars orbit
	October	—	Cassini mission to Saturn launched

APPENDIX 2: INTO THE FUTURE

The golden age of planetary exploration was in the 1970s, during the space race. Between 1970 and 1978 the USA and the Soviet Union launched thirty-one successful (and attempted many other unsuccessful) missions to other planets, not including the Moon. A loss of interest in space exploration and cut-backs in budgets meant that between 1979 and 1988 only nine successful probes were launched, and six of those were Soviet missions to Venus. The 1990s, however, have seen a return to the planets and a reawakening of our interest in exploring our Solar System (and beyond).

The ethos of planetary exploration has changed, though. It is no longer possible to spend huge amounts of money on massive, multi-purpose spaceprobes, building two of everything just in case one fails. The emphasis now is on smaller, faster and cheaper space exploration. The new generation of spaceprobes cost only a fraction (in real terms) of a 1970s probe, and are designed to do specific scientific jobs and to do them as efficiently and cheaply as possible. If a probe fails, it is not the disaster that it once was.

Since 1989 we have seen a new wave of explorers, many of which have featured in this book – Magellan, Galileo and Mars Pathfinder being the most important. The future, though, holds much more. Several important missions are already planned for launch between 1998 and 2006, and many more spaceprobes are in the planning stages.

The target of much of the planetary exploration in the first part of the 21st century will be Mars, certainly the most hospitable planet from our point of view. The goal for the near future is to put humans on the red planet. Five more orbiters will join Mars Global Surveyor over the next seven years, together with five landers and another rover. These explorers will search for information on the planet's past, look for evidence of life past or present, and pave the way to a manned mission which we hope will happen before too long.

A new area of research in the Solar System which will enjoy a burst of activity over the next few years is asteroids and comets. In the search for information on the early history of the Solar System, there will be two asteroid and comet flyby missions which will join NEAR and pass by a further five asteroids and comets. In addition there will be three missions to sample and return portions of a comet's nucleus to Earth, and one to return samples of an asteroid.

The rest of the Solar System has not been forgotten. The Japanese in particular are very interested in the Moon, seeing it as a possible stopping off point for the manned exploration of the Solar System, and are planning three lunar orbiters. ESA plans to return to Mercury with a probe that should go into orbit about the innermost planet in 2008 or 2009. NASA wishes to study Europa in more detail with a special orbiter which will determine the thickness of the icy crust, and find liquid water if it exists. There are also plans to visit Pluto for the first time, followed by a journey to the Kuiper Belt of comets beyond.

APPENDIX 3:
EXPLORING THE SOLAR SYSTEM ON THE INTERNET

The advent of the World Wide Web has created a host of interesting astronomical sites for the general public. As so many people have access to the Internet, either through PCs at home and work or through Internet Cafés, we decided that a list of some of the best sites on the Internet would be of use.

NASA
http://www.nasa.gov/
What more need we say? This is the NASA homepage from which it is possible to get to all parts of NASA.

Planetary exploration timeline
http//nssdc.gsfc.nasa.gov/planetary/chrono.html
A (very nearly complete) list of past and future planetary spaceprobes, with information on and pictures from many of the missions, and links to the homepages of famous, recent and ongoing missions.

NASA Photo Gallery
http://www.nasa.gov/gallery/photo/index.html
A list of links to picture collections throughout NASA and associated organisations. For images of the planets, try the 'Planetary Photojournal', while 'Welcome to the Planets' has all the information you could ever want about the planets and their moons.

SOHO homepage
http://sohowww.nascom.nasa.gov/
The home of the SOHO satellite has lots of information for the layman about the Sun as well as a great picture gallery.

INDEX

....

Page numbers in italic refer to illustrations